INTEGRATED INVESTING

Meg,
Fellow author!
Best of luck
with your Integrated
Investing journey.

Holeymyy

IMPACT INVESTING WITH HEAD, HEART, BODY, AND SOUL

Bonnie Foley-Wong

INTEGRATED INVESTING

BEVEL

Bevel Press
Vancouver, BC, Canada

Cataloguing data available from Library and Archives Canada

ISBN 978-0-9953274-0-5 (paperback)
ISBN 978-0-9953274-1-2 (ebook)

Produced by Page Two
www.pagetwostrategies.com
Cover and interior design by Peter Cocking

16 17 18 19 20   5 4 3 2 1

For more information visit:
integratedinvesting.ca
piqueventures.com

For my parents, Robert and Janet Wong,
who took risks and invested in me.

For my daughter, for whom
I'm trying to create a better future.

CONTENTS

INTRODUCTION

T HE WAY WE think about investing needs a reboot. Traditional economic theory assumes that the ultimate goal of business is profit maximization; since the 1980s, the focus has been on maximizing shareholder value.

The term "impact investing" was coined in 2007 as a way of describing a new way of thinking about investing. It seeks more than just financial outcomes from an investment, and more than just profits. With the development of impact investing, investors started to seek opportunities that not only had positive financial outcomes but also positive social or environmental returns.

To achieve different outcomes, however, we need a different starting point, and we need different tools for evaluating and acting upon investment opportunities. That's where integrated investing comes in. I developed this system to provide investors with the unique starting point and tools we need to really make a positive impact with our investment activities.

A Perfect Storm

Throughout this book are references to the 2007–8 financial crisis and the global recession that ensued. Eight years on, it is still strong and present in our minds—a benchmark against which we compare our decisions, actions, and performance.

Economic cycles are not new, but the boom that ended in 2008 demonstrated how complex and interrelated our financial systems are on a global scale. Is it a coincidence that the phrase "impact investing" was coined at a time when the world's financial and economic systems were about to enter a period of turmoil? Not everyone prospered during the boom time, and not everyone suffered great losses in the recession that followed. There has been a growing sentiment around inequality in the last seven years, and a number of books and research papers have been published on the subject of income and wealth inequality, including *The Spirit Level* (2009), a Michael Norton Harvard study on wealth inequality (2011), and *Capital in the Twenty-First Century* (2013), among others. Another visible signal of things being not quite right was the Occupy Movement that sprang up in the fall of 2011.

As these conversations emerged, I started to think about the systems and processes at play. I have worked in the finance industry through-out my career, and I learned in great detail how money moves through markets and how people make investment decisions when I worked in investment banking during the economic boom between 2003 and 2008. This experience, combined with my love of breaking things down into basic principles, led me to develop integrated investing.

This approach started with the realization that people benefit from integrating analysis, emotion, body, and intuition into their investment decisions. This idea goes against conventional thought, which says that analysis is the only input necessary for investment decisions, and that the best decisions are rational ones. But if that is the case, why do we continue to have significant social and economic issues globally, and why is income and wealth inequality worsening?

With the starting point of integrated decision making, I soon realized that to successfully implement integrated decision making and impact investing, we need a supportive environment and these things:

- An end goal: To what end are we making integrated investment decisions? We want to have a positive impact, but what is that impact? Don't we all want to survive, thrive, and be happy?

- Conditions: What motivations and mindsets set us up to make integrated investment decisions?

- Maps: How do values help us make decisions?

- Practical tools: How do we put integrated investment decision making to work? How do we gather the information we need to make an integrated investment decision?

Integrated investing is a holistic approach that encapsulates the end goal, conditions, maps, and practical tools needed to put integrated decision making into practice.

Beyond Being a Good Consumer

Many of my friends and colleagues try to shop ethically, sustainably, or locally. They can do so because they have multiple options available to them when it comes to purchasing decisions about clothing, food, and gifts. However, options are still limited when it comes to investing decisions. Credit unions may present a better alternative for banking and financial services, but when it comes to getting advice about investing and the investment products themselves, there isn't much variety available.

Maybe you have experienced a similar problem. You might purchase products from a local designer, craftsperson, or small business owner, but you don't feel equipped with the right techniques and tools to invest in those businesses. You might care about a particular cause, and the companies that your mutual funds are invested in may actually be contributing to the problems your cause is trying to address. You might run your own business with a set of values, but don't know how to make those same values feature when you make investment decisions.

This book will help you think about investing differently, take the first steps toward making a positive impact with your investment dollars, and understand the new trend called impact investing.

Who Am I?

When I was a child, my parents, who were fairly risk-averse at the time, saved money on my behalf and purchased government savings bonds. Once I started working and graduated from university, I started to save and invest my own money. Until I developed integrated investing, my own investment portfolio looked rather average. I never felt I had the time to study companies on the public stock exchanges, so I invested in mutual funds. As a new graduate fresh out of university, I sought help from my sister's financial advisor. Later, when I moved away from home to another country, I found my own advisors.

Having a career in finance and getting educated in the investment industry certainly changed my perspective on investing, but the evolution has been gradual. When I started to understand the dynamics of business, economic systems, and markets, I started to choose the mutual funds I wanted to invest in and instructed my financial advisors to fulfill those transactions. But after the financial crisis of 2007-8, I became disillusioned with the public capital markets and my portfolio of mutual funds. I couldn't see how my mutual fund investments could deliver the financial or social impact returns I wanted.

I believe there is a fine line between poverty and wealth, and it has to do with access to education, information, and the skills for making good decisions. Education was a game changer for me. It got me my first job during and after university, and it got me to London, one of the financial centers of the world. I set about educating myself about how investing could be done differently. This education led me to impact investing, and then to creating integrated investing.

In 2012, I started to develop my new approach and in parallel, developed Pique Ventures, an impact investment and management company that provides fund development services for impact investors and through which I provide services as a senior executive in the investment industry. I also founded Pique Fund, an impact venture fund that invests in early-stage startup companies that aim to generate both financial and social impact returns. Integrated investing is the investment methodology that I put into practice every day in both my business and the fund. My goal is to help people access the knowledge, information, and skills to make impact investing decisions effectively and confidently.

In This Book

Integrated investing's foundational pieces start with a concept of impact I developed called **access to essential resources**. In Chapter 1, I introduce the six categories of essential resources we need to survive, thrive, and be happy. Essential resources are the products, services, and activities that we need to fulfill our wants and needs. I talk about how businesses exist to give us access to essential resources, and why businesses provide different levels of it.

In Chapter 2, I explore **why we invest** in the first place. Our reasons influence how and in whom or what we invest, and often lead to more questions and more information. In this chapter, I look at the definition of investing, describe how where you are in life affects your readiness to invest, and share with you eleven purposes of investing and how they relate to the six essential resources.

Integrated investing is part of a new field called **impact investing**. In Chapter 3, I talk about the emergence of impact investing and how it connects with the impact concept of access to essential resources. I then describe the qualities that make an investment opportunity an impact investment.

Values affect decisions in your life. In conventional investing, a specific set of values has been foisted on investors. In Chapter 4, I discuss how your personal values can be introduced into your investment activities, and how to make investment decisions that align with your values.

A radical new way of making investment decisions, **integrated decision making**, is introduced in Chapter 5. I walk you through how information from analysis, emotion, body, and intuition not only affects our choices, but is also essential for making decisions in the face of uncertainty. I also share techniques for integrating analysis, emotion, body, and intuition into investment decisions.

Integrated investing requires certain conditions, so in Chapter 6 I talk about six **mindsets** that are important for a new approach to investing and investment decision making. Grouped into three categories, these affect your perceptions about resources and risks, influence your outlook on how to relate to and interact with others, and affect your frame of mind about results.

In Chapter 7 I introduce the **integrated investing toolkit,** practical tips and tools that can be applied to identify and evaluate impactful investment opportunities. I cover traditional analytical tools and practices, contemporary tools adapted from lean startup tools, and my own impact evaluation tools.

The **integrated investment relationship and resources,** discussed in Chapter 8, are designed to help you get started and find opportunities where you can hone and practice your integrated investing skills. I walk you through some places to start investing, how to start building investment relationships, and some of the common forms of investment.

In the final chapter, I share a specific application of integrated investing. From my own perspective and experience as a woman in the investment field, I discuss **gender lens investing**. I discuss gender equity and inequity, explain what gender lens investing is and why it is important, and what you can do to invest with a gender lens.

Making a decision about an investment opportunity that has the potential for positive impact and financial returns is complex. This book will provide you with foundational concepts, information, and tools to help you make the decisions you'll be required to make throughout an investment experience. It covers analytical, emotional, physiological, and intuitive inputs that could influence your decision making so you start investing with head, heart, body, and soul.

1

ACCESS TO ESSENTIAL RESOURCES

IN 2007, I found myself at the pinnacle of my career while working for an investment banking team at a Dutch bank. I worked on some of the biggest, most lucrative commercial real estate financings in Europe, ranging from €15 million ($19.5 million) to €1 billion ($1.3 billion) in size. When I was headhunted for a sovereign wealth fund, it felt like a natural progression to make—from debt financier to equity investor. The sovereign wealth fund was backed by a significant amount of money, so much so that it was plotting a hostile takeover of a British supermarket company for a price of over $20 billion. The fund proposed to borrow over $12 billion to pay that price.

By this point in my career, these large deals had long since been reduced to numbers on a page. As a result, the customers who bought the food at the British supermarket company and the staff that worked there didn't feature in the deal analysis. I learned the hard way that the fund was not about innovation or solving real problems for people. Any attempts I made to think creatively about challenging and unusual opportunities were frowned upon. Any investment deals I put forward that did not fit the mold my bosses had in mind (an exaggerated version of borrow, buy, and flip quickly) were considered a waste of time. The work I was doing, and the kind of investments the fund wanted me to do, did not feel purposeful.

Problems in the financial sector were starting to brew in 2007. Interest rates were rising, and rumors of bank takeovers were rife. The Dutch bank I had been working for until May of that year was acquired by a Scottish bank shortly after I left. In November 2007, I left the sovereign wealth fund and, coincidentally, the fund abandoned its bid for the supermarket company amidst "the deterioration of credit markets," which is industry speak that meant that the cost of borrowing the money needed for the takeover had increased significantly and they did not think they could profit from the deal.

Leaving the sovereign wealth fund was a rude awakening. Working there was supposed to be a logical next step in my career, but instead it had turned out to be disastrous. The lucrative paycheck and the well-appointed London office they'd provided me with could not hide the fact that they characterized the problems in the financial and investment industry, and that the values upheld by the people working at the fund were at odds with mine. Years of cheap debt and fast deals were about to come to a crashing end. I had to get out, but where was I going to go? Career-wise, I felt lost.

I took this time to redirect my energy toward activities, businesses, and people that focused on innovating and solving real problems whilst working toward economic viability and sustainability. I concentrated my efforts on activities and subjects that interested me and that I had experience with. It led me to think carefully about why we invest in the first place, and about the role of finance and investment in today's society. I traced the path of investing back to the purpose of business and to the things we need in order to lead happy, healthy, and thriving lives.

In this chapter, I will share my insights and findings from my journey with you. These insights form the foundation of the investment approach I developed. In this chapter, you will learn the following:

- The six essential resources that we need to fulfill our wants and
  needs in life

- How businesses exist to give us access to essential resources
- Why businesses give us different levels of access to essential resources

Essential Resources Fulfill Our Needs

Since leaving investment banking and the sovereign wealth fund, I've spent a lot of time thinking about what makes us happy, what the purpose of business activity is, and how those two things may be connected. For people to survive, thrive, and be happy, there are certain things in life we all want and need. We need food to eat and clean water to drink to satisfy our hunger and thirst. We need shelter and clothing to protect us from the elements, and care, treatment, and remedies to protect us or treat changes in our health such as injury, illness, and disease. We need stories, images, and sounds to express ourselves and connect with others, and transportation to connect us from place to place. We need information from all sorts of sources to make decisions.

I took stock of all these things and summarized them into the following six categories of essential resources:

1. Sustenance: Essential resources to sustain ourselves
2. Expression: Essential resources to communicate and express ourselves
3. Connection: Essential resources to connect and develop relationships with others
4. Managing Change: Essential resources to prepare for or experience change or for managing change
5. Making Decisions: Essential resources for making decisions
6. Exchange: Essential resources for exchange

Some resources fall into more than one of these categories.

Essential resources are the things that we must find, access, process, and synthesize to survive, thrive, and be happy.

1. Sustenance

Sustenance describes things that maintain someone or something. Here are some essential resources we need to sustain ourselves:

- Food and clean water to satisfy our hunger and thirst
- Shelter and clothing to keep us warm or shaded and protect us from the weather and climate
- Energy to give us light and heat and to power other systems

Sustenance provides nourishment and satisfies our most basic physiological needs; therefore, it has a strong inward focus. It represents the essential resources that we need to ensure our own survival and self-preservation.

2. Expression

Expression is how we make our thoughts, feelings, and values known. We are a highly expressive and communicative species, using words, numbers, images, sounds, and texture to visually, verbally, and physically communicate with each other.

These are all forms of expression:

- Words and stories
- Numbers, charts, graphs, and ratings
- Images and design—art, photography, fashion, and style of dress
- Sound, music, and dance
- Tastes, smells, and textures

We also need essential resources of expression to communicate in different ways to a variety of recipients and audiences:

- Pen, paper, postal, and delivery services
- Telephone lines and mobile phone networks
- Newspapers, books, magazines, signs, and posters
- Radio and television
- Internet and social media channels

Expression starts with self and projects itself outward. It could go no further than your notebook or your room, or it could be shared with others. It represents the essential resources we need to convey our thoughts, ideas, insights, and feelings. Essential resources of expression enable us to communicate something about ourselves to others who have accessed the same or similar resources. We use these resources to communicate values, share culture, entertain, or evoke feelings.

This group of essential resources also includes design and aesthetics. For example, expression comes out in the style of our clothes, the products we use, and the cars we drive (or don't drive). Our values influence the choices we make around the products and services we use, and, in turn, the things we use reflect our values to others.

These essential resources of expression signal to others how we feel, what our preferences are, and what kind of journey we are on. We quote lyrics from songs and key lines from books and films. We wear art and fashion. These things tells others who we are and to what tribe we believe we belong. It is through these resources that we are able to express our feelings, ideas, and values.

3. Connection

Essential resources of connection enable us to build relationships. Connection is an interdependent, multisided interaction with other people and with nature (as contrasted with expression, which is more one-sided and centered on the self).

To fulfill our desire to connect with others, we need essential resources that enable us to do the following:

- Gather in pubs, town halls, community centers, hubs, and public spaces
- Network at events and meet-ups
- Transport ourselves in bikes, cars, planes, trains, and public transit systems
- Facilitate, invite, and listen in conversation

We are social creatures, and we thrive when we are able to form healthy relationships with other people and maintain a connection with nature. Much of what we do in work, life, and play happens in connection with other people. Sometimes we enjoy doing things by ourselves, like going for a walk, reading a compelling story, or daydreaming, but we are rarely alone in life. We encounter people on the street, in shops, or over the phone when we are purchasing other essential resources. We are never far from someone else with our smartphones and social media channels at our fingertips. We are more successful, satisfied, and happy with our connections when we have the resources to help us build those relationships.

4. Managing Change

We all experience change. Our bodies change as we grow and our circumstances change over time as we form partnerships with people, move, relocate, learn, and change directions. Things may happen to us unexpectedly or we may initiate it. We deal with change by preparing for it, experiencing it, and managing it.

Here are some examples of essential resources for managing change:

- Financial services and insurance help us deal with changes in our financial circumstances (or rather the financial consequences of changes in our lives).

- Travel enables us to experience a change to our surroundings, both voluntarily or involuntarily.

- Health care, often in the form of insurance, can help us manage changes to our health and the condition of our body and mind.

These are overlooked because we don't realize we are using essential resources as our circumstances are changing.

Change may be something that happens to us, such as illness, accidents, or something financial in nature, or that we initiate, such as relocation, pregnancy, or returning to school. It may be short-term and temporary, such as travel and taking a vacation, or long-term and more permanent, such as a union or marriage. All of these changes require resources.

5. Making Decisions

We spend a significant amount of our time making decisions, and often it feels like this is all we do. Simple decisions of the day may be about what to wear or what to have for breakfast. Bigger decisions in life that shape our path (or perhaps it is our path that shape our decisions) are about how and in what ways to further our education, where in the world to live, and what we want our livelihood to be.

Essential resources for making decisions can be as basic as what direction the wind is blowing, the position of the sun overhead, and the location of the brightest star in the night sky. We may obtain them from speaking with friends, family, and acquaintances who have information to offer based on their previous experience, or we may learn new tools through our own trial and error.

In the information age, essential resources for making decisions have become more prominent. Directories, Internet search engines, and smartphone apps aim to help us find what we are looking for. Products and services are reviewed by peers, friends, and complete strangers to help us make decisions that better suit us.

Information comes in many forms, and it is the integration of information from analysis, emotion, body, and intuition that enables us to make complete and whole decisions.

6. Exchange

We are not able to produce all our essential resources by ourselves—therefore, we need systems for exchange. The most familiar example is money. In itself it is not a useful resource, but when we trade or exchange it for the things we need and want, it becomes useful. Money, however, is not the only essential resource for exchange. Alternative currencies, community-based systems, and bartering can also be effective.

The Interconnectedness of the Essential Resources

Each one of the six essential resources is connected to the other five. We sustain ourselves to have enough energy and fuel for expression, connection, managing change, and making decisions. When we express ourselves, we communicate what other resources we have or need. We connect with other people and interact with them as we access those resources. We manage changes in our circumstances that affect how, when, and why we access other things we need. We make decisions about other essential resources and need them to exchange for other things we need or want.

How Essential Resources for Making Decisions
Relate to All the Other Essential Resources

Essential resources for making decisions are particularly important to our survival and happiness, so much so that it often feels like we spend almost all of our time on them. These are the most critical of all of the essential resources because they help us identify and find other things we need and help us choose among alternatives.

Sustenance: Our bodies tell us we are hungry and need food, but we need information to decide what to eat, how much, and how often. If the basic need of hunger is easily met, we make decisions about whether to grow and cook our own food, buy it from a farmers' market, local grocer, supermarket, or food wholesaler, or eat at a restaurant. Our bodies may feel cold as the temperature around us drops, but we must decide whether to wear a sweater, heavy coat, hat, or scarf to sufficiently keep ourselves warm.

Expression: We make decisions about how we want to express ourselves and in what medium to communicate our thoughts, ideas, feelings, and emotions. We decide whether to write a story, rate something on a scale of one to ten, paint a picture, tell a joke, or act something out using interpretive dance. Our decisions affect what we wear and how we decorate our homes.

Connection: We decide with whom we connect and how—with openness and invitation or with judgment and defensiveness. We make decisions about where we go to meet people.

Managing Change: We make decisions about how much change we can tolerate or actively pursue. We can decide to embrace adventure, quit our jobs, and embark on an around-the-world trip. We may decide that we require greater safety and security as we prepare to grow our family, have children, care for elders, or maintain our own health.

Making Decisions: This is where things get exciting and challenging. Essential resources for making decisions help us find and access more resources for making further decisions! As I mentioned above, essential resources for making decisions help us identify and find other resources we need and help us choose among alternatives. Although it may seem strange, that includes other essential resources for making decisions.

Exchange: We make decisions about what medium of exchange to use, how to get it, and what to spend it on. We must make decisions about whether to get a job or start a business to obtain money, the most familiar medium of exchange. We make decisions about whether to save our money, spend it, or invest it.

The decision to further our education—in school, through practical application, by attending workshops and talks, by asking others to mentor us, by reading books, or by observing others—equips us with additional essential resources like information, knowledge, and experience that help inform and shape how we will make decisions in the future.

This book, for instance, is a resource for making decisions—its content is designed to provide information and encourage a more integrated approach to investment decision making.

How Did You Get That Essential Resource?

Food as an Essential Resource of Sustenance
Food is energy for our bodies; we need it for sustenance. However, food meets multiple needs, and it can be a resource for things other than sustenance. Food is also a medium by which we express ourselves. We express our culture and our preferences through the food we eat and where we eat it. For some people, eating is a social activity. Meetings, conversations, and dates happen over food, making it a resource through which we can connect with other people.

Fashion as an Essential Resource of Expression
Fashion and our style of dress have long been essential resources for expression. What we wear expresses our mood, our tribe, and our culture.

Air Travel as an Essential Resource of Connection
Air travel—which includes the system of airplanes, companies, airports, and infrastructure—serves as an essential resource for connecting with others. It allows us to travel from one place to another to see and connect with people who live there. Sometimes people travel because they want to explore another land and culture. It was the idea of flight and long-distance travel that sparked the invention of airplanes—the desire to communicate

an idea, to connect with people, and to prepare for change. Over time, air transportation itself has had to adapt and evolve to the needs of people and the availability of different forms of essential resources. Concorde was the supersonic jet that first flew in 1969 and significantly reduced flying times between New York and Europe. Concorde made its final flight in 2003 as a consequence of rising fuel costs and a negative response following a major crash of one of its aircraft in 2003. As technology improved and laptops and mobile communications became common, people had access to different essential resources and were able to continue with their activities whilst on a regular flight, without the need to travel so quickly.

Financial Products and Services as Essential Resources for Managing Change

Banks and the financial products and services they provide exist to help us manage change. Financial products and services enable us to save money for a rainy day or proactively manage significant life changes such as education, buying a home, raising children, and looking after our elders.

Information as an Essential Resource for Making Decisions

When there is food, shelter, and energy available, as well as many other resources, you need to not only survive but also thrive. In this case, the one resource that becomes invaluable is information.

Increasingly, information is becoming one of the most sought-after resources. The business of collecting, mining, analyzing, and reselling data can be lucrative. In a time when technology has made the collection of data easy, processing it into meaningful information to assist people in their decision making is hugely valuable. I credit having access to information, as well as the skills and experience to filter, synthesize, and evaluate it, as one of the most impactful advantages I have had in life. Information about weather, rainfall, sunshine, and the fertility of a patch of land is important to a farmer. Information about the food we eat and the air we breathe is also significant. We seek information about neighborhoods, schools, businesses, and people to make decisions about where to live, our education and that of our family, where we buy things, and with whom we connect. Information as a resource for making decisions is an essential need, and businesses that give us access to information serve a critical purpose.

Purposeful Businesses Exist
to Give Us Access to Essential Resources

Businesses exist to give us access to all six essential resources, helping us to fulfill and satisfy our needs and live happy and thriving lives.

Business owners, entrepreneurs, advisors, and consultants involved in the building of companies frequently speak about the purpose of business as being able to solve a problem, meet a need, or relieve pain experienced by their customers. There is a direct connection between the vernacular in the business world and essential resources. When business people speak of solving a problem, they mean helping customers access essential resources.

Some businesses, which I call "purposeful businesses," help get essential resources into our hands. The following is not an exhaustive inventory of all businesses imaginable, but it should give you a sense of the types of enterprises that exist and the role they play. Notice how pervasive purposeful businesses are in our society and economic system.

Purposeful Businesses that Provide Sustenance

Essential resources of sustenance include food and clean water, which satiate our hunger and thirst, and shelter and clothing, which protect us from the elements.

Farm businesses, including large-scale industrial operations or smaller urban farms in your neighborhood, grow, process, and distribute food. Wholesale companies, retailers, restaurants, cafés, and fast food outlets help to bring the food to your table.

Businesses that treat, purify, and sanitize dirty water give us access to clean, drinkable water. There are also businesses that add and combine ingredients to make other products for us to drink and satiate our thirst.

We access clothing after businesses grow the materials, such as silk, cotton, or wool, or manufacture the materials, such as polyester, nylon, or Lycra. Along the production chain, businesses weave the materials into textiles, create, and deliver the garments. Retailers, including second-hand and consignment stores, sell the clothing to us.

Similarly, shelter in the form of houses and buildings exist after businesses harvest materials like wood, iron, and aluminum, or manufacture materials like plastic and vinyl. Businesses process materials, and they build, deliver, and manage properties. We access shelter after house-building and construction companies, property development companies, and property owners that rent buildings to tenants have played their part.

Purposeful businesses provide us access to raw materials and resources for processing, manufacturing, delivery, distribution, consumption, or occupation, all of which are essential resources of sustenance.

Purposeful Businesses that Enable Expression

Writing, images, film, fashion, art, music, food, fragrances, and other creative media allow us to express ourselves, our ideas, and our values to others. In this section, we focus on the businesses that make these essential resources of expression accessible to us.

Businesses exist to make, produce, display, market, distribute, and sell the books, images, fashion, music, food, and other media of expression. For art, there are galleries and art dealers. Literary agents, editors, publishers, printers, and online media producers make the written word in the form of books, magazines, or digital media accessible to us. Print-on-demand and social media platforms, themselves businesses, have emerged to enable artists and creators to self-produce and self-publish their own work. Music producers and retailers are businesses that give us access to recorded music. Live music reaches us via promoters, ticket sellers, and concert venues. Film and video reach us via producers and stores (in real life and online). Businesses operate movie theaters, produce, and distribute DVDs, and provide video streaming to our computers. All of these businesses and more make various forms of expression accessible.

Businesses incorporate forms of expression into products and services through design and style. With the decisions you make about the style of car, smartphone, soap, or coffee you buy, you are expressing something about your preferences and your values.

The feelings and ideas that you express and the messages that you communicate are delivered by telephone lines, mobile phone networks, and online networks, which are all operated by businesses.

Purposeful businesses provide access to the provision of materials, tools, conduits, platforms, and venues for essential resources of expression.

Purposeful Businesses that Enable Connection

The businesses that exist to help us connect with one another are diverse. Businesses enable us to connect in person, physically and virtually. Place-based businesses, such as cafés, bars, restaurants, conference centers, and community halls, as well as businesses that enable modes of transportation, make it possible for us to connect physically.

Businesses like Skype, Google, and online meeting service providers use Internet technologies to enable connection virtually. We are able to acquire skills and information around how to better connect with others from businesses that provide training in these areas.

Purposeful businesses give us access to the provision of places, media, transmission, communication, and transportation, which are the essential resources of connection.

Purposeful Businesses that Help Us Manage Change

We have businesses that provide products and services to address our need for financial security and to manage financial uncertainty and change. Banks, credit unions, mutual fund companies, investment firms, and insurance companies exist to help us accumulate and manage our money in case of changes in our financial situation.

Businesses in the hospitality and travel industry such as tour operators, resorts, and hotels enable us to voluntarily experience change. Moving and shipping companies help us manage change in our physical location. Health insurance, medical practitioners, counselors, therapists, pharmaceutical companies, and gyms exist to help us manage or influence change in our physical and mental health. Education businesses can provide us with skills and training in processes and problem solving tools for managing change.

Purposeful businesses that help us create a safety net and manage risk—be it financial resources, knowledge, or acquired skills—provide us with access to essential resources for managing change.

Purposeful Businesses that Help Us Make Decisions

The more we are inundated with information and choice, the more businesses emerge to help us make decisions. Search engines, business directories, and smartphone apps all help us access essential resources of sustenance, expression, connection, and managing change. Increasingly, businesses are being developed around algorithms that attempt to track and analyze behavior to predict a direction and help you make a choice. Businesses help map, curate, and match you with the essential resources you're looking for.

Education businesses and self-improvement courses also exist to provide you with the tools to make better decisions.

Many purposeful businesses provide us with the information, tools, map, or apps to find what we are looking for and help make decisions—they provide us with essential resources for decision making.

Purposeful Businesses and Money, a Medium of Exchange

As I mentioned earlier, the most familiar essential resource of exchange is money. Businesses are a conduit for money; they create jobs and transfer money to people in the form of salaries and wages. Businesses also put money into people's hands by purchasing goods and services from their suppliers.

A Word on Luxury Goods

If something is a luxury, it means it is not essential for our survival. Resources that meet a need of sustenance, expression, connection, managing change, and making decisions can be produced and packaged in forms that make them luxury goods. For example, caviar can be eaten, but it is not an essential form of sustenance. We have been encouraged to believe that extravagant diamond rings are an expression of a person's enduring love for their partner, but they are not essential. There are other ways to express love that do not require extravagance. Exclusive members' clubs are places where people can connect with each other, but they are not essential since there are other alternatives that are more inclusive. So yes, luxury goods exist; but I won't focus on them in this book, as they are not essential resources for us to survive, thrive, and be happy.

Purposeful Businesses Give Us Different Types of Access to Essential Resources

The difference a business can make in how the six essential resources are accessed can be described in one of six ways:

1. **Basic** access to resources
2. **Efficient** access to resources
3. Access to more or better **choices** of resources (greener, healthier, etc.)
4. More **convenient** access to resources
5. Through the **supply chain**
6. Through **employment**

Basic Access to Essential Resources

Some businesses provide basic access to essential resources. This is the first point of access: what you need when you do not have the essential resource you are seeking. It is, therefore, the simplest form, such as a roof over your head or food in your belly.

When you do not have basic access, you struggle to participate in society and in the economic system because you lack the energy and security to interact and exchange with others.

Efficient Access to Essential Resources

Over the course of history, businesses have harnessed the ingenuity and ideas in people's minds to invent machines and new technologies designed to make the manufacture and production of essential resources more efficient. Inventions such as the steam engine made it possible for businesses to mechanize and automate many hand production methods. This led to scale, and the essential resources we needed could suddenly be produced in larger quantities at a more rapid pace. The industrial era was the beginning of creating efficient access to resources.

With the advent of new technologies, efficient access to textiles, processed metals, mining and resource extraction, chemicals, machine tools, light and energy, glass, paper, agriculture, roads, rail, boats, and transportation was made possible.

Efficient access continued in the form of offshoring and outsourcing manufacturing and production processes in the 1960s and 1970s. Developments in computer technology in the 1990s began to enable outsourcing of services. Large-scale agriculture, mass production, and cheaper workforces have all been employed by businesses to provide us with more efficient access to essential resources.

More or Better Choices of Essential Resources

When businesses began to produce essential resources faster, cheaper, and more efficiently, it often meant they were using poorer-quality ingredients or materials, alternatives that were less healthy for us, or methods that led to the ill treatment of employees or the environment. As business owners recognized this, they created businesses to provide people more ways to access essential resources, thereby giving us more or better choices. These include organic food, such as fruits and vegetables, and organic materials, such as cotton. They also include business practices like fair trade, which ensures that farmers and workers are justly compensated, as well as accurate labeling of products.

Choice may also be about different technical or design aspects or different measures of quality and value. When businesses offer us more or better choices, we have different experiences of the essential resources, they reflect our values differently, and we may experience different price points. How we access essential resources may differ in terms of the choices provided by businesses.

Convenient Access to Essential Resources

When people have basic access to essential resources through an efficient means, and they have choices, businesses strive to enable convenient access as well. This can mean delivering essential resources to people's doorstep, or making them available nearby; it can also mean making them available quickly and in accordance to customers' time requirements.

Access to Essential Resources through the Supply Chain

Suppliers exchange one type of essential resource for money to access other items. For example, people who are able to produce fruits and vegetables supply them to a retailer in exchange for money, which they use to purchase fuel for their vehicles. By being part of a supply chain, suppliers can access other essential resources they need.

Access to Essential Resources through Employment

Similar to the way that suppliers get access to essential resources through the supply chain, other people get access through employment. They work to produce essential resources, and in exchange, they receive money that allows them to purchase other things they need. For example, a person who works for a cleaning business is paid wages as an employee, which enables them to pay their rent. In other words, employment gives them access to an essential resource of exchange and as a consequence of that, they are able to access an essential resource for sustenance: shelter.

What We've Learned

Everything we do in life falls into one of six categories: sustenance, expression, connection, managing change, making decisions, and exchange. We need essential resources to enable us to do them. In this chapter, we learned about the six essential resources that we need to fulfill our wants and needs in life. We also learned that purposeful businesses exist to give us access to essential resources, including the types of access I've called basic, efficient, choice, convenient, through the supply chain, and through employment. Now that we've covered these important concepts, let's delve into understanding and learning about the role of investing.

2

WHY WE INVEST

———————————

SINCE THE FINANCIAL crisis in 2008, I have spent a lot of time reflecting on why we invest, as well as what it means to do so. Why does the activity of investing exist? Do we need it?

I met Dougald Hine during my transition away from traditional investment banking and into the world of social enterprise and impact investing. Dougald is an author and entrepreneur and was named one of Britain's fifty New Radicals in 2012 by Nesta, a not-for-profit charity in the UK that focuses on innovation and helps fund the development and realization of new ideas. Following the significant shifts in the global economy in 2008, Dougald gave a talk describing five purposes of money, with the goal of helping his audience think about or move toward a way of living that was less reliant on money. He identified these five purposes:

1. Subsistence: A means to stay alive
2. Security: A means to manage your future, to make the world less unpredictable
3. Luxury: Something you enjoy but are not dependent upon
4. Status: Games by which people establish, hold on to, and change position
5. Accumulation: The idea that more is in and of itself better

Inspired by Dougald's ideas, but convinced that there must be more than five reasons why we invest, I delved deeper into our other motivations and identified eleven.

In this chapter, I look at the definition of investing, describe how where you are in life affects your readiness to invest, and go over the eleven purposes of investing and how they relate to essential resources.

The Definition of Investing

The word "invest" has origins from the post-medieval (1525–35) Latin word "investīre," which means to install, to surround, or to clothe in.

Dictionaries define the verb "to invest" as putting money to use for a return or accumulation, or to achieve an outcome. But money isn't the only way to do this; we can also invest our time, talents, and efforts.

For the purposes of this discussion, I define investing as **contributing resources, typically financial in nature, to businesses with the anticipation of generating long-term future benefit, outcome, or return**.

Where You Are in Life Affects Your Readiness to Invest

Since 2012, I've spoken with many people about impact investing in purposeful businesses that provide access to essential resources. These people sought investment advice and services across a broad spectrum, and I learned that knowledge and expertise in a particular subject matter, awareness of risk and impact, the skills of due diligence and scenario analysis, and the breadth and depth of their knowledge, awareness, and skills factored into their readiness as investors.

Another thing that factors into a person's readiness, of course, is where they are in their lives—whether they're new graduates, new or experienced entrepreneurs, already investors, or leaders in their respective fields. Ultimately, there are four stages a person can be in, categorized as follows:

- Safety: There are times when people find themselves focused on seeking safety and security, like when they feel resources are scarce.

For example, recently having graduated, having a baby, relocating to a new city, or undergoing some other significant change in life may require you to focus on saving your resources rather than letting them flow away from you.

- Building: Whether you are building a career or a new business, there is a point in every person's life—perhaps more than one—when they focus on gathering and collecting resources and applying them to something they are developing, or use them for their own self-development.

- Executing: After building, at a stage when we are confidently doing or executing, we begin to create surplus resources and start to find more room to help others.

- Leading: This is a stage when we feel resources are abundant due to success in our careers, our businesses, or our lives. At the leading stage, we find ourselves with more than enough time, expertise, and resources to be leaders, mentors, and to actively help others in the building and executing stages.

People in the safety stage are least likely to be ready to invest. They spend most of their resources on their day-to-day need, and if they are investing their resources it is to create a base or safety net and create a greater sense of security. People who are building are focused on investing in themselves or their own projects and initiatives, not in external ventures. The people who are in the executing or leading stages are in the best position to invest in others because they are equipped with the knowledge, insight, and resources to invest well and wisely. They have already invested in themselves and seen results; now they're ready to invest in something else.

Meet Some People at Different Stages of Life

Lynn is a new graduate looking for a financial advisor who can provide the advice she needs about saving money and what mutual funds to invest in, but who also understands Lynn's values and which types of companies she wants included or excluded from her savings portfolio. She is just starting her career. She is less concerned about investing in innovative new businesses, taking risks, and being a leader, and more concerned about learning, developing new skills in her job, and starting to save some money. Lynn is in the safety stage.

Karen is a mid-career entrepreneur who is two years into building her business. She is drawing on her experience, network of connections, and resources to make it grow. Although she has some savings, she is investing much of her residual earnings and available cash back into her business. Karen is in the building stage—not in a position to invest in someone else just yet!

Natalie has been running her business successfully for a number of years, and recently began to mentor other entrepreneurs. She combined some of her own money with that of a few friends and colleagues to make one investment in another business. A confident business owner, Natalie is relatively new to investing and is in the executing stage.

Suzanne is an experienced entrepreneur. She previously owned and operated a successful business that she sold to another company. She is also an outspoken community advocate and confident leader, and is already investing some of her own money in startups and growing companies. When Suzanne speaks, people listen. She is in the leading stage.

Yasmine is an example of how you can find yourself in different stages of life in relation to two different paths. Yasmine is a successful corporate executive and has experience raising investments for new ventures, as well as investing her own money. She is about to embark on a new startup venture, which means she is partly in the safety stage because she needs to give her venture enough resources to get off the ground amidst uncertainty. However, because she has budgeted well and has designated part of her money for her investment portfolio, despite the fact that she has her own startup to worry about, she is also keen to invest in other entrepreneurs and their ventures. She is also in the leading stage.

Although the stages of life are often sequential, progressing from safety to leading as you move through your career, that is not always the case, as we can see in Yasmine's situation. Throughout the course of your life, you could be in leading stage in one area, and then change paths and suddenly find yourself seeking safety and security.

Readiness to Invest and Taking Risks

Investing, by nature, requires you to take risks. The returns and compensation for investing are not immediate, and in many cases are uncertain. Not everyone is in a position to put time or money into something without a guarantee of remuneration or compensation in the future.

Investing and leading both require time, expertise, and resources. During the safety and building stages of life, people often cannot afford to take undue risks. People in the executing and leading stages of life, in contrast, can take risks as investors and steps as leaders to support the development of others who are not in a position to do so.

Investment capital can be used to pay salaries and wages (frequently of people in the safety and building stages of life) while a company is starting, building, and growing its customer base and revenues. It can be used for technologies, equipment, and other large assets that business operators do not have the excess resources to acquire. Essentially, an investor is someone an entrepreneur or business owner can partner with to take on whatever risk the owner—along with their employees and suppliers—can't afford to take on for themselves.

The Eleven Purposes of Investing and How They Relate to Essential Resources

As I mentioned earlier in this chapter, there are eleven reasons that people invest. These are status, power, leadership, connection, security, future consumption, preparation for obsolescence, innovation, legacy, making decisions, and exchange. All of these are derivatives of two primary reasons:

- To build businesses that enable people to access essential resources
- To directly access essential resources

Investing in Businesses to Access Essential Resources
As I illustrated in Chapter 1, purposeful businesses exist to provide access to essential resources. All businesses start with some form of investment—be it the founder's own time, resources, and money, or

that of an outside investor. Investing is critical for the formation and growth of purposeful businesses and therefore is a key activity to enabling access to essential resources for ourselves and other people.

Investing to Directly Access Essential Resources

We invest to build businesses to access essential resources, but there are direct relationships between investing and resources as well. Investing can directly provide the essential resources of sustenance, for example, if you invest in an income-generating asset and create an income stream. The income from your investing activities can then be used to purchase the resources needed to sustain yourself. Investing can also give you essential resources for expression, connection, and managing change. It also requires essential resources of decision making; these help you decide whether to invest, when to do so, in what or whom, with whom, and how much to invest.

Investing and Essential Resources of Expression

Three of the most prominent motivations for investment are status, power, and leadership—all three are forms of expression.

1. STATUS

Being able to say you were an early investor in a startup that later finds extraordinary success, or being a successful investor in any area, is a way to express status.

For some people, scouting talent amongst entrepreneurs holds great allure. People derive pleasure and satisfaction from spotting the next big thing, and in a competitive landscape, this is a win. Great enjoyment can come from making that new discovery and being the first investor; it gives you the feeling of having made something happen. People who are able to identify the "next big thing" get an elevated status. Their ability to identify stars gives them their own type of star quality. Exclusive early access to a company can also signify someone's social status, since they have to be connected to gain access to such excellent investment opportunities. Some people also find gratification in the status earned by investing in a business before it was cool or was adopted by the mainstream, or by investing in an iconic company.

Simply having the financial wherewithal to place a significant amount of money toward a risky business venture can also lend someone higher status.

The structure of securities legislation in most countries is such that angel investing in early-stage ventures is accessible only to people with high net worth and financial wealth. Venture investing has become an item of luxury. Recent changes in legislation and a movement known as crowdfunding are making venture investing more accessible, but in the meantime, investing continues to be a status symbol among the wealthy.

2. POWER

Power is the ability to do something or act in a particular way. Investors, with their power over their own financial resources, have the ability to create and grow businesses. Controlling businesses and the essential resources they provide can be an expression of that power.

If you control resources that people need to survive, thrive, and be happy, those people are at your mercy. By strategically investing in infrastructure, assets, and resources that are essential to human need, you gain control over who gets access to them, when, and at what cost. Conversely, lack of investment in some areas also controls resources, like in education, health care, and housing.

An idealist might say that impact investors are not motivated by power, but realistically, power dynamics are incredibly pervasive in the investment industry, even in impact investing. In my opinion, impact investing should be about shifting power over resources and the access to them so that power and access are more equally distributed, but this is not always the case.

3. LEADERSHIP

Investing to enable others to create and fulfill their potential helps an investor express leadership. Investors demonstrate informed risk taking, decisiveness, and a depth and breadth of experience and expertise that allows them to help others achieve their business goals. These qualities are the same qualities we often look for in leaders. In contrast to power, which is about empowering yourself, investing and leadership are about empowering others.

Developing Investors as Leaders

In 2013, in collaboration with a leadership development coach, I piloted an investor training program, working with seven professionals in the financial and business advisory industry. Each of our program participants expressed interest in learning how to grow from being a mentor to becoming an investor. They wanted to know how to apply their business expertise to advise startup entrepreneurs and help them realize their ideas and grow their ventures.

Our investors-in-training had a strong desire to help and empower others and solve problems through innovative new business approaches that featured elements of uncertainty and risk. They had the desire and ability to evaluate and take risks to help entrepreneurs deal with the uncertainty. With the new tools we taught them, our program participants were able to grow personally and professionally, and begin to express leadership in their field.

Investing and Essential Resources of Connection

Investing is an activity best done in the company of others. The fourth motivation for investing is for connection.

4. CONNECTION

Investing can be a connective and social activity in the form of investment clubs attended by like-minded people, and investors and entrepreneurs networking and connecting with each other at pitch events and other gatherings. Investment clubs have a long history; in fact, they have existed since the 1800s as a way to learn from other investors.

As an investor, you want to know who you are investing in; similarly, people who receive investments want to know who the money is coming from. Everyone involved in an investment—investors, entrepreneurs, and business owners alike—wants to know that it is in line with their strategies and objectives. This is particularly important for early-stage, angel, and venture investing.

Connection is an opportunity for investors to learn about what entrepreneurs need and what they have to offer. Likewise, connection enables entrepreneurs to learn what investors are looking for. By connecting, investors and entrepreneurs can start to build common understanding and empathy around each other's requirements and aims.

Investing and Essential Resources for Managing Change

The primary role of investing—given its orientation toward future benefits, outcomes, and returns—is to help us manage change. Unexpected change in the future can cause undue stresses and pressures on your life and others. Being well prepared for change can help reduce this.

Managing change can take different forms. It can be creating a safety net of resources that can be used in the future in case of emergencies, or it can consist of proactively setting aside reserves of resources to purchase the essential resources you'll need in the future or to prepare for current essential resources becoming obsolete. It can mean innovating and developing new forms of essential resources or ways of accessing them. Investing to manage change can also be about setting aside and growing resources for future generations.

5. SECURITY

We invest to enable security by accumulating reserves to manage an uncertain future and to compensate for the decline in human capital as we age.

The words "saving" and "investing" are often used interchangeably. You might save money for a large purchase or expenditure in the future, to buy a home or car, or to pay for a significant travel experience or for something important in the future for your children or dependents. Or you might save for a rainy day to ensure you'll have access to resources in case of an emergency.

You might also set aside money for a time in the future when you will be earning less or no money from working. Saving for your retirement may be a familiar purpose of investing. As we age, our ability to generate income—or at least our energy for it—declines. So we invest, setting aside resources now so that they might grow and be available if we need to draw upon them in the uncertain future.

Those people who are motivated to invest out of a desire for security generally set aside enough for their day-to-day living expenses and then earmark the remainder as money they can save and invest.

You could stash this money under your mattress, of course (and some people do), but you are more likely to put it to use on an investment product, through your bank account or investment account, that pays you a financial return in the form of interest, dividends, or capital gains.

6. FUTURE CONSUMPTION

We invest to enable future consumption by accumulating resources that can grow and multiply, knowing that those augmented resources can be used in the future.

Investing for future consumption requires the deferral of immediate gratification. We hope and anticipate that investing today will yield more in the future. Investment growth requires a number of factors to work in concert; however, there is a risk involved here. If one or more conditions are not right, the investment might not yield anything, and you may even lose the original investment entirely.

7. PREPARATION FOR OBSOLESCENCE

We prepare for obsolescence by investing in replacements or improvements. As things fall into disuse, wear down, or grow out of date, they become obsolete. An asset becomes obsolete when it is no longer economical to keep it in use, even if it is not yet physically worn out.

Older cars can still transport people from one place to another, but their relative fuel inefficiency, polluting effects, and evolving carbon emissions regulation prompt investments in newer, more fuel-efficient cars. As oil becomes more expensive and scarce, all petroleum-fuel vehicles will eventually become obsolete, paving the way for newer technologies such as electric vehicles, and uses of alternative fuels (all of which require investment).

Victorian buildings in London, England, sturdily built in the late 1890s and early 1900s, feature rabbit warrens of rooms and corridors. These floor plans don't work for many businesses today, which demand bigger spaces with fewer walls and partitions (open-plan office spaces). As the needs of businesses changed, those older buildings of brick and concrete were demolished to make room for glass and steel structures that offer more space. This is one example of how we invest in things to create alternatives as things become obsolete.

8. INNOVATION

We invest in innovation as we anticipate change. Humans have a high propensity for creativity and planning. We innovate to create things that improve comfort, convenience, and efficiency in our daily lives and activities. Sometimes we innovate to address serious social and environmental issues, or just for novelty. Investing in a new venture may be an investor's search for the authentic, novel experience.

As we anticipate things becoming unsuitable for our purposes, we innovate. Perhaps we are running out of a resource or raw material, or maybe we want to be able to do something faster, in greater quantities, or less expensively. Such goals require us to innovate, and by extension, to invest in innovation.

9. LEGACY

We invest in legacy by creating wealth for future generations. A legacy is created by investing and accumulating assets that will ultimately be left to someone else. As a purpose of investing, this serves several different objectives: looking after future generations, caring for or serving others, or as a way of being remembered once you have passed.

Investing and Essential Resources for Making Decisions

Investing involves a series of decisions—why, how, how much, in what or in whom, when, and for how long. Investing requires information, knowledge, and know-how. These are all essential resources for making decisions, but access to essential resources for making decisions is also a motivation for investing.

10. MAKING DECISIONS

One of the outcomes of investing can be new information and tools for making decisions. You learn new things through the activity of investing that can help you make decisions in other areas of your life or you could invest in a purposeful business that creates essential resources for making decisions. Examples of businesses that make information or tools for making decisions include Google (search tools to help you find information), Yelp, and TripAdvisor (directories of places, including user reviews about where to go to shop or where to stay on holiday). B Lab is a business that manages the B Corporation certification system, which sets a standard for social and environmental performance, accountability, and transparency of businesses. The B Corporation certification is information produced by B Lab to help people make decisions about the companies they do business with, shop with, or invest in.

Investing and Essential Resources for Exchange

Lastly, a motivation for investing is the essential resources that result from the activity of investing that could be used for exchange. These include the investment asset itself, in the form of shares in a company or some other form, or its financial outcome.

11. EXCHANGE

When investing activities produce a return, it can give you access to an essential resource for exchange. Typically, the return is a financial one, but some innovative and alternative investment structures might also pay you a return in-kind, meaning you receive your investment return in the form of a tangible product. If you are able to trade that product for other resources that you want and need, you have still received a resource for exchange as a result of investing.

Investments themselves take the form of equity shares in a company or a loan, which are collectively referred to as financial instruments. In some situations, financial instruments could also be exchanged for other essential resources.

As an Integrated Investor

Use these questions to reflect upon the reasons why you want to invest.

- Are you seeking a return from your investing activities for sustenance?
- Do you require a steady investment income stream to enable you to purchase the essential resources you need?

- Is making money from your investments a primary concern? Why or why not?
- Does the status of being an investor appeal to you?
- What do you wish to express about yourself by being an investor?
- For what do you want to be remembered as an investor?
- What kind of change are you interested in influencing with your investing activities?

What We've Learned

The motivation to invest is the important first step to investing. Determining why you're investing is the first decision you make in your journey. In this chapter, you learned about the foundations of investing, including its definition and why we invest in the first place. Investing is not only necessary to the survival of businesses that provide access to essential resources; it also gives you access to essential resources of sustenance, expression, and connection, and for managing change, making decisions, and exchange.

3

IMPACT INVESTING:
TAKING CARE OF THE VILLAGE

THE BURSTING OF a housing bubble. Financial institutions' significant exposure to sub-prime lending. Complicated financial
derivative products. These are just some of the things that led to
the great global recession that began in December 2007. In September
2009, the Organization for Economic Co-operation and Development
(OECD) cited improved economic activity in the world's eleven most
significant economies—the United States, United Kingdom, Germany,
Italy, France, Canada, Japan, Brazil, Russia, India, and China—and thus
announced the end of the global recession. But that was certainly not
an end to the socioeconomic challenges the world faces.

Occurring in parallel with the global recession and continuing
well past 2009, many people expressed growing dissatisfaction with
the financial system and public investment markets. Alongside this
emerged an increasing desire to address those socioeconomic challenges whilst investing, or at least make investment choices that did
not cause or worsen those problems. Many of my friends, associates,
and colleagues complained of lack of transparency and value in their

investment choices. They felt their investments were not impacting their local communities, or their communities of common interest or cause, in a positive way. But most of them did not know where to turn or what to do about this. Many were changing how they shopped when it came to products and services like food, clothing, and other consumer items so that their purchases aligned more closely with their values. Many were also changing their jobs, livelihoods, and career paths to be better aligned with those feelings. But few knew what to do about their savings and investments; those were locked away in the opaque, complex financial system they felt incapable of untangling for themselves.

In 2007, impact investing emerged as a prevailing solution for a more purposeful approach with the intent of addressing some of the negative social and economic impacts arising from traditional approaches to investment decision making. But this new form of investing is not without its challenges. Even now, as impact investing is starting to break into the mainstream, it is often as opaque and complex as conventional approaches.

In some cases, practitioners and companies in the burgeoning impact investment sector have started to apply financial and investment models, processes, and approaches borrowed from the very system that collapsed in 2008, which is a frustrating revelation. Applying conventional investment approaches to purpose-driven companies or businesses with a social mission embedded in their business model is not the solution.

In this chapter, I peel back the onion layers of impact investing by getting back to basics about impact investing and drawing the connection between it and access to essential resources. First, I share from where impact investing emerged, present three ways of describing what "impact" is, and explain why impact is, by nature, personal.

The Emergence of Impact Investing

The new approach to investing that emerged in response to people seeking a more positive alternative to conventional approaches goes by many names. I will use the term "impact investing" to broadly describe this field, which is often also referred to as social investment, social finance, triple-bottom-line investing, values-based investing, and mission-related investing.

In 2007, the Rockefeller Foundation convened a meeting "to explore with leaders in finance, philanthropy, and development the need for, and ways and means of, building a worldwide industry for investing for social and environmental impact." At this meeting, people started to use the phrase "impact investing," and so it was coined. This was a big deal. The White House announced a national impact investing initiative in June 2013. The description of impact investing included the movement of capital toward businesses, with the intention of generating economic return as well as benefit to the public. It was seen as a concept whereby businesses measure environmental, social, and governance (ESG) considerations in addition to measuring financial returns. The White House also referred to commonly used terminology such as "shared value" and "social enterprises."[1]

What Is Impact?

In Chapter 2, I proposed a definition of investing: contributing resources, typically financial in nature, to businesses with the anticipation of generating a long-term future benefit, outcome, or return. But where does "impact" come in?

Impact is connected to the access to essential resources and can be described in the three following ways:

- Empowering people and the planet and not exploiting them
- Creating more equal societies
- Taking care of the village

Let's go over these in detail.

---

1 Elizabeth Littlefield et al, "Announcing the National Impact Initiative at the UK's G8 Social Impact Investing Forum," The White House Blog, June 7, 2013, accessed April 8, 2016, http://tinyurl.com/WhiteHouseImpactInitiative

Empowering People and the Planet

Impact investing is investing in businesses that through their value proposition, relationships, and business practices empower customers, employees, suppliers, and other stakeholders. Impact investing works with businesses that do not exploit people and the planet, and is itself never exploitative.

As we discussed in Chapter 1, the essential resources we need fall into six categories:

1. Sustenance (examples: food, clean water, shelter, energy)

2. Expression (examples: through speech, writing, creative, and artistic endeavors, in what we wear, and through our culture)

3. Connection (examples: we meet in person, we talk over the phone, we travel to see each other)

4. Managing Change (examples: information, bank accounts where we can save for a rainy day, insurance)

5. Making Decisions (examples: information, decision-making tools)

6. Exchange (examples: money, alternative currency, barter goods)

People become more empowered when they have the essential resources to sustain and express themselves, connect with others, manage change, make decisions, and have a means of exchange. When people have improved access to the essential resources they need to do the things in life to survive, thrive, and be happy, more equal societies result.

Payday Loans: Helpful or Exploitative?

Consider a situation in which you have the opportunity to invest in a new company called MoneyGrabbr. The company loans money to people with poor credit histories and credit scores who would otherwise not be able to borrow from a bank. MoneyGrabbr has a convenient website through which its customers can specify the amount they want to borrow and for how long. It would cost $69 to borrow $300 for fourteen days, meaning an annual rate of 599.64%.[1] MoneyGrabbr loans are known as payday loans because the money is lent to the customer in advance of a payday and is intended to be repaid with the next paycheck. However, customers often find themselves short of cash on payday, making meeting their current financial demands and paying off the loan from the previous pay period impossible. Customers who are unable to pay down their loans when they become due often renew their loans or borrow more, creating an endless cycle of borrowing.

A company like MoneyGrabbr can potentially be a lucrative investment opportunity, as the recurring interest revenue it generates can be significant, but payday loan companies are often criticized for exploiting cash-strapped customers.

Then a company called LoanSaver comes along. It also loans money to people who have difficulty accessing loans from banks, but it only does so if the customer can set aside a small amount of money as security for the loan. That loan security is placed into a savings product. The intention of LoanSaver is to help its customers learn how to grow their savings and manage their money more responsibly. An investment in a company like LoanSaver has the potential to yield a financial return, since, similar to MoneyGrabbr, it grows its revenues through the interest it collects. Unlike MoneyGrabbr, however, LoanSaver also creates positive social impact by helping its customers break out of the cycle of depending on high-interest short-term borrowing like payday loans. LoanSaver not only gives its customers access to essential resources of exchange (money), but also to managing change (savings) and making decisions (education around managing their finances).

―――

Impact is about empowering people, and people are empowered when they have access to essential resources. We are able to influence impact through our investment decisions, including the choices we

―――――――――――

1   Based on an actual short-term lender in British Columbia, Canada, where there are maximum fees for short-term lending. In other countries, the cost of a short-term, payday loan may be even higher. In the US, payday lending is legal in twenty-seven states, with nine others allowing some form of short-term storefront lending with restrictions.

make about which businesses get started and grown, and about how businesses are led, managed, and operated, and how they serve people. When determining whether something is an impact investment or not, the differentiating question is, "Does the business exploit people and the planet or empower them?"

Creating More Equal Societies

Also in Chapter 1, I talked about how businesses enable people to access essential resources. Impact happens when businesses enable a change or improvement in how essential resources are accessed:

- Basic access: People who do not have access, gain access (examples: shelters for homeless people, affordable housing for people on low incomes, agriculture systems for communities on the brink of starvation)

- Efficient access: People who already have basic access are now able to access resources more efficiently (examples: wide-scale agriculture for more efficient production of food, larger distribution systems, replacement of one-to-one tutoring with schools for more efficient delivery of education)

- Choice: People who have basic and efficient access now have choice in the type of resources they access (examples: fair trade, organic products, buying local rather than buying products mass-produced overseas)

- Convenient access: People who have basic and efficient access now have convenient access (examples: smartphone apps that help people find the nearest coffee shop, stores with the products and services you need, when you need them in close-by locations, ordering products online that are delivered quickly to your door)

- Employment: People who can access essential resources for exchange (money, in the form of wages and salaries) or some of the other types of essential resources (free room and board, for example, provides someone with essential resources to sustain themselves)

- Supplier: Ethical sourcing and purchasing is another way to give others access to essential resources (such as sourcing coffee beans from a cooperative, organic coffee producer in Peru, sourcing clothing wholesale from factories that pay a living wage, or buying fresh produce from a local, urban farm that hires people from the local community who experience barriers to traditional employment)

Giving someone luxury access to resources—that is, giving people at the basic, efficient, choice, and convenient levels further access to resources in excess (luxuries)—does not create more equality. In fact, it has the opposite effect by increasing the inequality gap.

When I talk about impact, I focus on changes in access that relate to basic, efficient, or choice access. For a business that provides people with convenient or luxury access to products and services to be considered positively impactful, it must be the source of improvements in people's access to essential resources through employment or the supply chain. For example, inclusive hiring policies that create jobs for people who have experienced long-term unemployment, who are homeless, or who have disabilities improve access to essential resources through employment. A coffee-grinding business that sources its coffee beans directly from farmers and ensures that they are fairly compensated improves the access to essential resources for the farmers through the supply chain.

> Inequality is typically measured in terms of income, but it really means differences in people's level of access to essential resources. Inequality affects people at the bottom end of the wealth spectrum the most, but it also affects people at the top.

Richard Wilkinson is a British researcher who focuses on social inequalities. He retired from teaching in 2008, is Professor Emeritus of Social Epidemiology at the University of Nottingham, and is the coauthor, with Kate Pickett, of the book *The Spirit Level: Why More Equal Societies Almost Always Do Better.*

Wilkinson believes we intuitively know that rising inequality gaps (measured by relative income) are a problem. Through his extensive research, he unearthed data demonstrating how more equal societies are healthier and happier. Using metrics such as life expectancy, math and reading literacy amongst children, infant mortality rates, homicide rates, proportion of the population in prison, teenage birthrates, levels of trust, obesity, mental illness (including drug and alcohol addiction), and social mobility, Wilkinson's research evidenced that more equal societies had **higher**

- life expectancy,
- literacy rates amongst children,
- levels of trust,
- social mobility.

His research also demonstrated that more equal societies had **lower**

- infant mortality rates,
- homicide rates,
- proportion of the population in prison,
- teenage birthrates,
- obesity,
- mental illness,
- drug and alcohol addiction.

Using the data available on the health and social problems listed above, Wilkinson and Pickett formed an index of health and social problems for each country and each US state. Each item in the indexes carries the same weight, and the higher the score, the worse the outcome. Countries with low inequality, such as Japan, Finland, Norway, and Sweden, scored better on the index of health and social problems, whereas countries with high inequality, such as the US, Portugal, and the UK, scored the worst.[1] American states with low inequality and better index scores included Utah, New Hampshire, and Wisconsin. At the other end of the spectrum, with high inequality and worse index scores, were Louisiana, Alabama, and Missouri.[2] Although the US state data

---

1   Richard Wilkinson and Kate Pickett, *The Spirit Level: Why Equality Is Better for Everyone* (London, Penguin, 2010), 20.

2   Wilkinson and Pickett, *Spirit Level*, 22.

scatter widely around the trend line, the correlation between inequality and the index of health and social problems is clear.

In *The Spirit Level*, Wilkinson and Pickett note a correlation between trust and inequality. They noted the highest levels of trust amongst people in the Scandinavian countries and the Netherlands, countries where the income inequality gap is small. For example, in Sweden, 66% of the population noted that they feel that they can trust other people. Contrast that with Portugal, where only 19% of the population said the same. Differences in income in Portugal are high.[1]

Although a number of factors besides inequality affect women's status, Wilkinson and Pickett found, using measurements by the Institute for Women's Policy Research, that it tended to be worse in US states with high inequality, including Louisiana, Alabama, and Missouri. In more unequal states, women earn less, and fewer women vote, hold political office, or complete college degrees. Comparing different countries, we see that a number of factors influence women's status, but there is an unmistakable, visible trend toward women having lower status in more unequal countries.

Improving Wages: Living Wage and Income Equality

The MIT Living Wage Calculator noted that low-income families in many parts of the US do not make a living wage. That is, many families do not make sufficient income to afford the high cost of living in their community.[2] In countries around the world, campaigns have been launched to encourage businesses to pay each of their employees a wage sufficient for an employee to meet their basic needs, or to encourage policy makers to establish laws requiring a living wage. Although basic needs may differ somewhat from country to country, they include subsistence such as shelter (housing), clothing, **and the basics for quality of life**—food, utilities, transport, health care, and some recreation. Education, family care (children and elderly), saving for retirement, legal fees, and insurance may or

1   Wilkinson and Pickett, *Spirit Level*, 52–53.

2   Living Wage Calculator, accessed April 8, 2016, http://livingwage.mit.edu.

may not be included. The MIT Living Wage Calculator provides a useful illustration comparing the minimum wage, poverty wage, and living wage across different family compositions based on location. The living wage in a given place is typically significantly higher than the minimum wage, especially for adults supporting a family with young children. An investment in a company that adopts a living wage policy could be considered an impact investment because such a company is attempting to give their employees improved access to essential resources, and possibly shrinking the income inequality gap.

In April 2015, Dan Price, CEO of Seattle-based company Gravity Payments, took reducing income inequality a step further. He announced that he was setting a minimum wage of $70,000 for all of his company's employees. The policy will be phased in over the course of a few years, and Price is cutting his $1 million salary down to $70,000. In a city where the cost of living is higher than the US national average (24% above the national average, according to PayScale, mainly due to the high price of housing), Price made the decision to adjust the minimum wage in his company in a bid for greater income equality among the employees. In an article in *Time*, Price talked about hiring and retaining talent based on providing an opportunity to serve others and grow in their roles, not just an opportunity to make money.[1] His approach echoes one of my strong beliefs—by taking the issue of money off the table, staff worry less and can focus on work. When people are living paycheck to paycheck, it can be distracting. Because its bold policy on income equality is an attempt to empower its employees, an investment in a company like Gravity Payments could be considered an impact investment.

Investing as Taking Care of the Village

"Taking care of the village" means doing things that take care of us, our families, our neighbors, our communities, future generations, and our planet. It is the idea that to have a happy, thriving life, we really must

---

1   Farnoosh Torabi, "Why This CEO Pays Every Employee $70,000 a Year," *Time*, April 23, 2015, accessed April 8, 2016, http://time.com/money/3831828/ceo-raise-70000-dan-price/.

realize that we are interdependent and that operating in isolation is not good for our well-being. It takes a village to do the things that matter.

In a village, there are multiple stakeholders whose interests must be met, and there are future generations who will inherit it from us.

This means making investment decisions with the village in mind. It means evaluating whether the people we invest in have the same aim and mindset, and it means assessing whether the businesses we invest in serve the goal of taking care of the village. In this approach, we choose to invest in businesses that meet our needs and those of our families, our neighbors, our communities, and future generations, while also taking good care of our planet.

Investing with this mindset is different from seeing it as an extrinsically rewarded game, which is what business and many things in life have been reduced to. We think game play is a good motivator or incentive structure, but this is where negative consequences can arise. Games can be manipulated, especially where they are primarily extrinsically rewarded. Investing as a game is characterized by people aiming for high scores (higher and higher investment returns and business valuations, and chasing more money for themselves for its own sake) and knocking all their opponents off the playing field (creating greater inequality). This leads to less regard for other people. Investing as an extrinsically rewarded game puts us at risk of forgetting that real people are involved.

Taking care of the village puts the intrinsic motivation back into our activities and people back into focus.

> **Investing as taking care of the village also empowers a diverse community of people to invest in businesses and make decisions about their future. If we do not have diversity among investors, we perpetuate the same systems that have resulted in more unequal societies and the exploitation of people and the planet.**

Investing as a Game

Leading up to the 2008 economic crisis, I was working in an industry that had financial models coming out of its ears. It was a highly measured and numbers-centric environment. We only focused on five things: the size of the deal, how much money we could make, how much money we could place in the capital markets, how much each banker was going to make in salary and bonus, and how much the people next to us were going to make.

Although we made numbers on computer screens get bigger and bigger, our activities actually created little value. We shuffled the numbers from financial institutions to our clients and back again, and the only thing we succeeded in doing was to make rich people richer. People pursued making lots of money so they could spend it on things that compensated for their unfulfilling work. Some bankers were like robots—living without purpose, chasing bonus payment after bonus payment, and spending more and more extravagantly at bars and restaurants, on properties, and on vacations. It was an expensive form of escapism and a never-ending pursuit. Bankers caught in the rat race sought things that made them feel good, but they were all superficial. These were highly extrinsic rewards.

Titles and goals achieved, listed with some monetary or number value attached to them, are shortcuts people often use to quickly form an opinion or assessment about someone else. But if no attention is paid to the actual value created, they remain shallow. Whenever I see people comparing their title or rank with others or think about people pursuing higher salaries, higher valuations, or bigger deals, it reminds me of the games you can find in the app store: win that badge, complete that level, get a higher score.

Leaving the conventional banking world prompted me to explore how approaching investing as a game could lead to people and the planet being exploited and the inequality gap widening. This led me to try to figure out what impact investing was about and make sense of the state of the investment world, and as I did, several questions came to mind:

- Is investing in ethical, responsible businesses a more natural way of investing, or is investing just to make more money innate in people?

- Why don't all investors insist on higher standards of business ethics and the fair and ethical treatment of suppliers and workers? Why do people make investment decisions that lead to the insensitive and unsustainable plundering of the earth?

- Why is investing with the sole purpose of making lots of money and then giving some away as charity or philanthropy the predominant approach to doing business and doing good? Why is the prevailing purpose of investing making more money?

I don't have all the answers, but I do know that while returns are important, not everyone invests solely to make more money.

Striving to get the highest score motivates people to focus on maximizing profit and endless growth. It motivates people who believe that more for its own sake is better, ignoring who gets more, who is not getting more, and worse yet, who is getting less. It also motivates people to cut costs, since that will lead to greater profit—an approach that can lead to the planet being exploited and the long-term cost of environmental harm not being accounted for or being pushed onto someone else (such as future generations or countries where environmental laws may be more lax). Cutting costs can also mean someone in the supply chain being exploited, getting less, or being treated unfairly.

A focus on knocking all the competitors off the playing field or beating the other team creates an us-versus-them mentality.

Investing as a game causes the profit-motive to become unhinged from the purpose-motive, and participants to become more distant from the fact that businesses and investment decisions affect real people. Profit becomes a way of keeping score and an end rather than a means of taking care of the village.

Our current economic and financial system rewards people who play the game. Investment industry professionals place too much emphasis on metrics that reward game players—people constantly looking for rational reasons and measurable evidence to support the investment decisions being made. The rules and predominant culture of investing lean in favor of this approach. People who have earned high incomes or have significant financial wealth can more easily play in the investment game. Smart, entrepreneurial, creative people who have not played the game and lack the same kind of scorecard are left out, despite the fact that they have experience, expertise, and insights to contribute.

The investment industry fails to sufficiently acknowledge how vital trust, insight, foresight, emotion, intuition, and culture are because they do not find these decision influencers reliable. A vicious cycle results from this failure—one that depends upon game-like metrics and rewards game-like behavior, and discounts the importance of behavior that takes care of the village.

We need to change how we make decisions about investment because of the important role it plays in determining what businesses exist, what products and services are available to us, how we are employed or make a living, and ultimately how we get access to essential resources.

How to Take Care of the Village and Avoid the Bad Games When You Invest

There is a type of investment game playing that is particularly damaging to our societies and to our economies in the long run. I encourage you to learn how to spot it so you can avoid unknowingly participating in the game and instead invest with taking care of the village in mind.

The kind of game playing I'm talking about is when an investor uses a business in which they have invested as a game piece, and bases all their decisions on trying to maximize their score and knock all their opponents off the playing field (measured by their return on investment and beating out other investors).

Indicators that someone's investing is driven by an extrinsically motivated game-playing approach include the following:

1. They appear to have invested solely to make money and maximize their own gains, rather than to create value, no matter the cost to people and the environment.

2. They place too much emphasis on numbers and metrics, and ignore how people feel about a business, as well as the impact it has on people when evaluating the business's success.

3. They exhibit a lack of awareness of intuition, emotional intelligence, and empathy.

4. How they behave in their business dealings is not the same as how they behave in personal relationships.

5. They actually refer to investing and business as a game.

For example, someone investing in an advertising business that bombards people with ads for things they don't really need is focused on profiting from people blindly spending and excessively consuming products and services. Someone investing in a payday loan business, like MoneyGrabbr, the example described earlier, is focused on profiting from people becoming trapped in a never-ending cycle of dependency on expensive debt.

Investing as taking care of the village, in contrast, is an approach that appreciates collaboration over competition, creates real long-term value for people and the planet, respects the needs of all people in the village, and plays a part in providing the resources needed to meet everyone's needs. In contrast to someone who sees investing as a game, someone taking care of the village will invest in a business in the sharing economy, thereby repurposing and getting the full use out of products and services that otherwise sit idle. Given the choice between investing in a payday loan business and investing in a lending business that helps people save money and break out of debt dependence, an impact investor will choose the latter, regardless of whether the first is more lucrative.

Impact Is Personal

The "impact" in impact investing reflects how we feel when we, or others with whom we empathize, are healthy and happy. We can identify positive impact by the emotions of happiness, elation, or contentment. Positive impact can also elicit a feeling of satisfaction or being at peace with ourselves and others.

Our experiences and stories about impact tend toward an emotional response. We feel moved when we get improved access to essential resources or witness other people getting improved access to essential resources for sustenance, expression, connection, managing change and making decisions. Traditional investing approaches were built upon mainstream economic theories from the late eighteenth and early nineteenth centuries, all of which stated that a business's primary goal should be profit maximization, decision making should be based on one's self-interest, and rational decision making should be dominated by reason and analysis. Investors were told not to let emotions affect their decisions.

Some of the common emotions that researchers frequently cite as being dangerous in investment decision making include herd mentality, loss aversion, and fear of regret. What I believe to be missing from much of this research is how positive emotions that are not rooted in fear can positively affect an investment decision. When I have made major decisions in my life from a proactive place of positive emotion, rather than one of fear or a desire to avoid negativity, I experienced great outcomes. Given this, why do we not take positive emotions into consideration when investing?

In the 1970s, Milton Friedman promoted the idea of increasing shareholder value as the primary purpose of business, which set an easily measurable goal for businesses and motivation for investors. Some people were able to make a lot of money using this model, and therefore maximizing shareholder value became the predominant focal point of investment. Any idea of other forms of value creation—such as equality in societies and the empowerment of people—fell by the wayside. That left impact as the traditional focus of charity and philanthropy.

Charity and philanthropy, however, are not the only ways to have impact. Investing in purposeful businesses can also be effective. This isn't necessarily a new idea, but it does harken back to times before maximizing shareholder value became the investment world's focus. Investing in purposeful businesses is now more complex, with supply chains and customer communities spanning the world. This is why we need a different, more integrated approach, and a toolkit for making purposeful investment decisions.

Barbara Stewart, a portfolio manager who advises wealthy individuals and families, asked one hundred women how they spend their personal time, energy, and money and published her findings in her 2013 white paper "Rich Thinking." Here are some of the personal causes her interviewees focused on:

- Ensuring we all have water that is safe to drink
- Sustainability and addressing climate change issues
- Access to career development resources for unemployed, reading-challenged people

- Responsible leadership
- Providing electricity in fast-growing, power-deficient communities
- Access to education for young girls in India
- High-quality architectural design that really serves people
- Technological advancements that benefit economies for present and future generations
- Mentoring women on challenging work and life issues
- Childcare and development for orphans and vulnerable children
- Investing in companies and helping them solve problems, be more efficient, and create a better future for everybody
- Receiving or providing legal services in a more efficient and accessible way
- Health and medical innovations
- Justice and opportunities for women
- Working toward social justice through microfinance services
- Offering wisdom, advice, and inspiration to people on challenging personal and professional journeys
- Helping others make their ideas happen
- Diagnosing and treating cancers
- Spending time in the community in social services, arts, and education
- Helping people reconsider overlooked spaces in their communities and appreciating how our physical environment tells a story about our communities and culture
- Supporting entrepreneurs and entrepreneurship as an investor
- Creating a women's running series—runs by women for women
- Issues of social and women's justice
- Preserving the privacy of our personal information

This is a long list, but it is by no means exhaustive. That's the point: the diversity in the number of causes and types of impact that are possible demonstrates that impact is personal.

Causes and what people believe to be impactful in the world are as great in range as they are in diversity. However, they all have something in common: each of these causes relates to access to essential resources.

Thinking of impact in terms of improvement in people's access to essential resources will help you make the transition from a mindset of charity and philanthropy to one of purposeful business and impact investing. This is the foundation of integrated investing.

Summary

There is more to life than just numbers. When we ignore words, narratives, and stories that evoke emotion, we ignore significant factors that affect our decisions. We ignore the intuition, gut feeling, hunch, internal whispers—whatever you want to call them—that help us navigate uncertainty and chart direction for the future. Investing is a complex activity that should involve all these things.

Impact investing is about contributing resources, typically financial in nature, to businesses with the anticipation of generating long-term future benefit, outcome, or return to increase and improve access to essential resources for you, your family, your neighbors, your community, and future generations. Impact is the improvement in access to essential resources, which empowers people, protects the planet, and creates more equal societies. Investing as taking care of the village succinctly captures this idea of impact.

4

INVESTING WITH YOUR VALUES

WHENEVER WE MAKE investment decisions, we are asked about our financial situation and appetite for risk, but not often about our values. Values are a representation of the compass by which we guide our decisions, and yet investment advisors tend to focus only on issues such as your bank accounts, what kind of insurance coverage you have, your savings for education, your financial net worth, your pension, and your retirement savings. When investment advisors do ask non-financial questions, they ask about hobbies and lifestyle, not about your values.

In 2007, I decided I wanted to align my personal investment portfolio more closely with my values, so I worked with a financial advisor to put my money into mutual fund investments. At the time, I thought socially responsible investment funds (SRI funds) were the only alternatives available to me that could reflect my values. I inquired about SRI funds with my financial advisor, but the conversations were short-lived. She typically directed me away from them, telling me they generated inferior financial returns compared to other funds. But financial return was not the only thing I was interested in. I wanted to invest in companies that were responsible, innovative, and demonstrated good leadership. To me, that translated into investing in companies that encouraged good stewardship of our planet and environment (like renewable energy companies), rather than those that exploit, pollute or cause damage to the environment (like oil and gas companies). It also meant companies that treated their employees fairly, empowered people, and promoted leadership diversity. Following the advice of my financial advisor meant that my personal investment portfolio did not reflect these values.

Frustrated by both my financial advisor's lack of interest in values-aligned investing and the lack of nimbleness large, publicly traded companies afforded me in terms of changing my investments to reflect a more holistic set of values, I turned my attention to private companies without the support of my financial advisor. The misalignment between my values and the large companies I'd been dealing with, and my feeling of being unable to influence positive change in them, led me to integrate values into my work and to create more investment choices for other people who also wanted to invest in a values-aligned way. Since then, I've found that investing in private companies gives investors the opportunity to make choices that are more closely aligned with people's values.

In Chapter 4 we will dig deeper into what investing with your values means. Investing involves a number of key decisions, and as I mentioned above, values help guide our decisions every day, in particular the major decisions in our lives. In the pages that follow, I will show you how values do the following:

1. Help you figure out how to decide
2. Influence your motivation to invest in the first place
3. Guide what broad areas or types of companies you should invest in

How Values Help You Decide

A value is something that makes sense to you and that you feel good about. They are present when you apply your intuition and make decisions. When we ignore our values while making decisions, we end up with results that don't make sense to us or that we feel unhappy with. We find ourselves going down a path that feels off track. This couldn't be truer where investment decisions are concerned.

If you think about the things in life that you really care about, do your investments reflect them? Your values represent the important things you care about and stand for, but do you invest in businesses that produce, provide, or do the things that reflect them? For example, say one of your core values is healthy eating and maintaining a healthy lifestyle. Why would you then invest in a company that produces and promotes high-fat, high-sugar, low-nutrition food? Or perhaps you value local economic development by supporting small businesses and manufacturing. You wouldn't want the bulk of your investments to be in companies that do all of their manufacturing abroad, would you? In both of these examples, if you invested in the businesses described, your investment choices would not align with your values. More values-aligned investment choices would be companies that produce and promote healthy, organic, nutritious food, or local manufacturers and producers.

The first step toward values-aligned investing is to develop a greater awareness about your values and how you can make investment decisions that agree with your core values. Your investment attitudes, behaviors, and activities simply should not be at odds with what you believe in.

One of my core values, for example, is fairness. When I encounter a situation where people are being treated fairly, it makes sense to me from an analytical standpoint. I feel good about fairness. It evokes a positive emotion. I intuitively sense that fairness is a good thing, and I believe it will serve me and others well in future interactions and endeavors. When I experience being treated fairly or witness it with others, I physically feel good—I might even feel positive tingles. If I come across a situation and I can identify fairness in it, I am able to make a decision more quickly. Contrast that with a situation where people are not being treated fairly. Analytically, I know that unfairness is not sustainable in the long run, and witnessing unfair situations makes me feel incensed and agitated. Because of this, I know I want to invest in companies that treat people fairly—including their customers, suppliers, employees, and investors—and I strive for fairness in my own negotiations with companies and entrepreneurs.

> **If integrating analysis, emotion, body, and intuition into decision making is the long form, aligning your values with your decisions is the short form.**

If you ever encounter a situation where you need to make an investment decision and are unsure what to do, and reflecting upon your values doesn't make it any clearer for you, that is when the tools and techniques of integrated investment decision making will come in handy.

How Values Influence Your Motivation to Invest in the First Place

The first thing people ask me when they are thinking about investing is, "What should I invest in?" But the first question they should be asking is, "Why am I investing?"

In Chapter 2, I talked about the motivations for investing. The first steps is to look at your motivations. Knowing what your values are will help you answer this question.

Using your values to determine why you are investing, rather than blindly following fads or echoing other people's reasons, is more likely to result in a satisfying experience—not to mention outcomes that match your expectations.

Here's an exercise to help you apply your values in deciding why you are investing. First, let's review the list of possible motivations from Chapter 2:

1. Status
2. Power
3. Leadership

4. Connecting with others
5. Security
6. Future consumption
7. Preparing for obsolescence
8. Innovation
9. Legacy
10. Resources for decision making
11. Resources for exchange

Which of these motivations represent your current reasons for investing?

Whereas motivations are the reasons you have for acting in a particular way, values are your principles or standards of behavior, or your judgment of what is important in life. It is possible to be motivated by something that is incongruent with your values. The following validity and completeness tests are designed to help you develop better awareness around your values and how they affect your investment decision making. They can help you to make decisions that are more aligned with your values.

Take a look at the list of motivations again. Which ones reflect your values? I call this the validity test because it gets you to check whether your motivations to invest accurately reflect your values. For example, is it power that motivates you to invest? If so, is power something you value?

Now, try the completeness test. Keeping your core values in mind, look at the list of motivations again. Are there any that better reflect your values and are missing from the list of your current motivations for investing? How do you feel about why you are investing? Do you have feelings of dissatisfaction or doubt, even if it's just a nagging feeling in the back of your mind? These could be signs that something is amiss.

Let your decisions and actions as an investor reflect your core values. If your motivations for investing are not aligned with your values, the outcomes certainly won't be aligned either. If your motivations are aligned with your values, then you have a good foundation for making investment choices that you will feel good about, even proud of, and that will make sense to you.

List of Values

For example, I value the following:

1. Abundance
2. Curiosity
3. Discovery
4. Education
5. Fairness
6. Honesty
7. Integrity
8. Leadership

I believe my resources are sufficiently abundant to invest some of them. I value curiosity (so much so that I named my investment and management company Pique Ventures—as in "pique your curiosity"), and I have a healthy tolerance for risk because I am curious about the unknown and embrace uncertainty with curiosity. I value discovery, and this shows up in my propensity to invest for innovation and helping others discover new things. I particularly value education because I believe that it is the reason I have had access to so many opportunities and have been able to tackle challenges in life to survive, thrive, and be happy. I value fairness, honesty, and integrity as well, and therefore I look for these values in the entrepreneurs and opportunities I invest in. Lastly, I am motivated to invest to demonstrate my role as a leader and influence positive change.

How Values Guide the Types of Companies You Should Invest In

In Chapter 1, I introduced the concept of access to essential resources. In deciding what to invest in, ask yourself what types of resources and access you value. You can do similar validity and completeness tests by comparing the types of resources and access against your list of core values and vice versa.

When you are evaluating a business as an investment opportunity, the validity test asks whether the essential resources provided by that business align with your core values. The completeness test poses the question of whether your core values are present or evident in the essential resources provided by the business under evaluation.

Aligning Your Values with Essential Resources

Let's consider some examples of how values align with essential resources and how you can use values-alignment to guide your investment decisions. If your core values include survival and security, it might be important to you that you and all people have access to the things needed to survive. If this is the case, then you may be drawn toward essential resources for sustenance like food, clean water, shelter, clothing, and energy, which means you're more likely to want to invest in businesses that enable access to these things.

If you value creativity, essential resources for expression may fit with you. This could draw you toward investing in businesses that value art, music, dance, or design. One of the areas of focus in my investment work is the creative economy, where creativity and expression are integral to a company's products and services, and where the business model is wrapped around the core values of creativity and expression. These include ventures such as independent film and multimedia, written content, and businesses in the fashion industry. In my case, I particularly look for businesses that encourage positive body image, individuality, and imagination, because these are things that I also value.

Your values may also align you with essential resources for connection. If this is the case, you may decide to invest in businesses that value cooperation, collaboration, and friendship. One of the businesses I work with is called myBestHelper. It helps families connect with and find caregivers (babysitters and nannies). It is more than just a transaction-based business; the founder of the company recognizes that finding a trusted caregiver is like welcoming a new member of the family into the fold, and that resonates with me and my values. Connection (between families and caregivers) is the essential resource provided by myBestHelper and is a core value for the founder, the company, and its investors.

People who value change, adventure, control, or discipline may invest in different businesses that provide access to essential resources for managing change. Other similar values include predictability, pragmatism, structure, stability, wealth, and accumulation. If these are important to you, look for investment opportunities in businesses where they show up not only in the value proposition, products, and services they offer, but also in how they do business.

Information, education, and decisiveness are key values that show up in businesses that value essential resources for making decisions. If these are some of your core values, investing in businesses that reflect them would make sense for you.

You might value fairness, equality, and equity like I do. These might be expressed as a business's fair employment or supplier practices, or in how the business treats its stakeholders. Alternatively, this might show up in a business's attitude toward money, or it might appear in a barter-based business model. One of the more recent themes in business and investing is the rise of businesses in the sharing economy, like Airbnb, TaskRabbit, and myBestHelper.

Values of justice and inclusion may lead you toward businesses that provide basic access to essential resources. Investments in microfinance institutions (locally or in developing countries) and affordable housing are examples of businesses that reflect the values of basic access.

Many businesses focus on business models that increase efficiency or expediency. Investors that value efficient access to essential resources are often attracted to these kinds of investment opportunities.

Another theme amongst investment opportunities focuses on offering people choice and alternatives (such as organic food and drinks or fair trade and more ethically produced goods and services). If you value choice, abundance, fairness, and health, then investments in businesses that provide access to a choice of essential resources may align well with your values.

If you value convenience or ease, businesses that provide convenient access to essential resources may be right up your alley. These include businesses that are able to reduce drudgery, automate repetitive tasks, or scale their operations such that you can access them conveniently (online, from your mobile smartphone, on every street corner, or where you do your business or shopping).

If justice, fairness, inclusion, and work are important to you, business that provide essential resources for exchange—for instance, businesses that have fair, inclusive, and ethical hiring policies and supply chain practices—may be the types of organizations you want to invest in.

Values Exercise

Figuring out what your values are takes self-reflection and self-awareness. It is not about what your values should be or what other people believe. It is about what is important to you.

If you already know what your values are, jot them down and keep them on hand. You will refer to them as we delve further into what investing with our values looks and feels like. If you are not sure what you value the most, then take some time to contemplate this.

Identifying Your Values

Go through a list of values and categorize them into three groups, in the context of what is important to you in investing and investment decisions. Rank them as very important, important, or not important.

A list of one hundred values is shown below. Please add you own as well. A longer list is available at www.listofvalues.com. It is worth it to be comprehensive and go through a long list to see what resonates with you. There are some words on the longer list that describe the same thing, but one word might mean more to you than another. Identify as many values as are important to you.

Abundance	Consistency	Diversity
Achievement	Control	Dominance
Advancement	Cooperation	Education
Adventure	Courage	Endurance
Belonging	Creativity	Entertainment
Celebrity	Curiosity	Equality
Change	Decisiveness	Equity
Collaboration	Delight	Experimentation
Communication	Design	Faithfulness
Competition	Discipline	Fairness
Conformity	Discovery	Fame

Familiarity	Learning	Safety
Family	Loyalty	Scarcity
Flexibility	Money	Security
Freedom	Nonconformity	Self-respect
Friendship	Openness	Sharing
Fun	Order	Speed
Generosity	Passion	Spirituality
Growth	Patience	Stability
Harmony	Peace	Status
Health	Persistence	Structure
Helpfulness	Play	Surprise
Honesty	Pleasure	Wealth
Hope	Perfection	Wisdom
Imagination	Power	Status
Improvement	Practicality	Thoughtfulness
Individualism	Pragmatism	Tolerance
Innovation	Predictability	Tradition
Integrity	Purpose	Trendy
Inclusion	Recognition	Trust
Insight	Reliability	Utility
Inspiration	Resilience	Wealth
Justice	Responsibility	Winning
Leadership		

After you have ranked all these values for yourself, select the eight values that matter most to you. If you have trouble prioritizing, use a grid available at www.beverlyryle.com/prioritizing-grid to help.

Tell Your Story to Identify Your Values

Another way of recognizing which values are most important to you is to write stories about situations or events from your past that are meaningful and identify the values that are present in the stories.

The importance of family, frugality, and hard work were instilled within me by my parents from early in my life. Hidden within the auspices of family cohesiveness were the values of love, interdependence, and connectedness. I learned that constant learning and curiosity was how I would pave my path of personal growth and development. Through my own mistakes, failures, and accomplishments, I learned that love, trust, and honesty, with myself and with others, were things that I valued. As I got older, I started to reflect upon what I had learned, what I was curious about, and how my interpersonal relationships had developed. I reflected upon aspects of my life where love, trust, and honesty were prevalent.

I had all my basic needs met as a child. There was a roof over my head and food on my plate. I had supportive parents and teachers who encouraged me to excel in school. I had access to education and health care. Our communities were safe. We had access to transportation, both public transit and cars. The fact that I had access to all these resources meant that I was able to concentrate on learning, spending time with my family, and having fun.

I've come to realize that we all generally abide by similar values, even though we express them differently and place varying importance on them. We are all generally pursuing the same goals as well, just on different paths, and have different methods by which we use information to make decisions along the way.

STORY EXERCISE

Think of five to seven times in your life when you were motivated to effect change or speak out about something. Write about moments in your life when you have been most moved to take action —out of passion or love or anger or frustration—or when you wished you could take action. Or write about a burning issue that is currently on your mind. Reflect on these stories and examine the values that were present in the choices you made. Look for the attitudes and behaviors that you exhibited in these situations. As you do, you may see patterns or themes emerge. It's also possible that each story will highlight a different value.

Write two or three lines describing each situation you come up with. Consider these things as you write:

- What was the decision you had to make, or the change you wished to effect?
- What obstacles did you face?

What things, including feelings, experiences, or advice, helped you make a decision? Try to trace back to earlier lessons in life or to values or principles that were passed on to you by your parents, elders, mentors, or other people that influenced you.

Refer back to the list of values and see what values you recognize in your stories and in yourself. Now can you narrow your list down to eight core values?

Test Your Values

If you have not spent much time thinking about your core values (and most people do not), these exercises might feel a bit unusual. When anything feels new or unfamiliar, it is helpful to test things out, wear them for a while, and see how they fit. Put your decisions to the test against your values and see if they stand (are keepers) or if they fall (need revisiting or relegation). Your list of core values might change after you have had the chance to reflect upon them. This doesn't mean that your values have changed, but rather that their prioritization or your awareness of them may change.

In the next chapter, we'll dig deeper into how to make integrated investment decisions that also align with your values.

5

INTEGRATED INVESTMENT
DECISION MAKING

I WAS EXPOSED TO saving and personal finance early on in life. My parents helped me open a bank account when I was a child, and I invested my meager savings in national savings bonds.

As a teenager, my education was well-rounded. I tried my hand at all sorts of subjects, including science, mathematics, creative writing, music, and visual arts. But when it came to choosing a career path at the end of high school, I decided to become an accountant because I was good with numbers. I also remember thinking that the world would always need accountants.

I studied mathematics in university and majored in accounting, and later earned a post-graduate degree. I even learned how to code, as computer science was a significant component of the math faculty in my university. I can't say I recall having much exposure to investing during my university years other than a course on corporate finance, the real-life application of which I wouldn't realize until much later on in my career.

My studies landed me a job with a global accounting firm, where I spent my days auditing financial information and meeting with finance teams and chief financial officers of entrepreneurial companies.

Working for a global accounting firm opened the door to Europe. I relocated to the UK with my firm, and there I first had exposure to mergers and acquisitions, private equity, and corporate finance. I became a corporate finance advisor in London, working with and advising entrepreneurs who were buying companies, selling them, or raising finance. But after a couple of years of advising and recommending, I wanted to understand investment decision making better. I wanted to get up close with investment capital, and be directly involved in the decisions about how it would be invested.

My desire to understand the investment decision-making process in greater detail became a driving force in my career. This guided me toward investment banking, and later to where I am now—designing, building, and leading new venture funds and applying a more integrated approach to investment decision making for both myself and my clients. I am excited and passionate to share what I know about integrated decision making with others because it's a better, more holistic, purpose-driven approach that anyone can apply to their investment activities and benefit from in the form of financial, impact, and social returns.

Integrated decision making is linking, coordinating, and combining inputs and information from multiple sources to choose a course of action, including analysis, and your emotions, body, and intuition. Integrated investing specifically applies decision making to the activity of investing and combines motivations, mindsets, and tools for yielding integrated investment returns.

We are at a turning point in the economy and society, when the old approaches to investment decision making have failed us. To embrace a new idea or concept requires us to let go of analysis, just for a moment. Suspend your disbelief that investment decision making is only about analysis. We must also engage emotion and intuition, and pay closer attention to our bodies, to make sound investment decisions. In the absence of all other information, integrated decision making is where you start and what will help you make decisions even when facing the most complex investing dilemmas.

For example, you could apply integrated decision making when you meet an entrepreneur and learn about their venture, and you are evaluating whether or not it is an investment opportunity you [...] pursue. This specific point in the investment decision-makin[g] already has a lot of complexity. At this point you're wondering if you like the entrepreneur, whether you can work with them and their team, whether the venture is going to succeed in having a meaningful positive impact, and whether it will be economically viable and profitable.

Integrating information from analysis, emotion, body, and intuition will help you answer these questions more quickly and confidently.

In this chapter, we'll go over the parts of the integrated decision-making process, which include the following:

1. How analysis helps us decide
2. How emotion affects our investment decisions and how greater emotional awareness can actually help us make better decisions
3. How our bodies can affect how we approach risk or stress and therefore affect investment decisions
4. How intuition is necessary for making investment decisions in the face of uncertainty
5. How to integrate analysis, emotion, body, and intuition into investment decisions

Once you have a better understanding of the integrated decision-making process, you'll see why it is so effective.

How Analysis Helps Us Decide

Analysis is probably the decision-making input you are most familiar with. It involves formulas, metrics, measurement tools, numbers, and ratios that are pegged against some benchmark in such a way that they can help you decide whether an investment is worthwhile for you or not.

We use four analytical tools in investing: count, calculate, compare, and contrast. For example, the number of years in business and number of customers are counted. Revenues, margins, profits, and ratios are calculated. Entrepreneurs and companies are compared and contrasted to others that you've read about, that you've worked with previously, or that you've met recently.

It can be tempting to compare a company's current revenues and profits to those from previous years, or to those of other companies, but with early-stage ventures, there is limited information on revenues and profits (or if there is information, the results from the early years are often lumpy and inconsistent). Instead, we try to analyze other information we can count, such as the number of customers, or we try to analyze the entrepreneur's record of success from previous companies and ventures.

Sometimes we compare and contrast an entrepreneur to others we know. We look at their credentials, degrees, and professional designations. We compare and contrast the number of years they have been working or the number of businesses they have started and exited.

What Analysis of Businesses Tells Us: Examples

The following are examples of three investments made by the impact venture fund Pique Fund, based in British Columbia, Canada. This isn't the only analysis we did. We also analyzed past financial statements, future forecasts, and projections. The following gives you an idea of the types of analysis we did.

Wearable Therapeutics—At the time of Pique Fund's investment in Wearable Therapeutics, the founder had already sold a significant number of the company's product, Snug Vest. Although the company was not yet profitable at that time, its revenues could be measured. Snug Vest is an inflatable vest, a wearable technology that enables users to experience a form of deep pressure therapy. Analysis of the number of children and adults with autism who had purchased Snug Vest gave us an indication of how many people Wearable Therapeutics was able to help. A quick analysis of the competitive landscape showed that there were a number of businesses aiming to serve a similar customer base.

Beanworks Solutions—Beanworks provides accounting workflow automation software. To analyze the opportunity for Pique Fund, we looked at the number of invoices processed by the software and growth in invoices processed. We also examined the number of customers, signed users, customer growth and retention rate, and new business generated through referrals. We had sufficient data to analyze the largest customers. The CEO also committed to at least a 50% female workforce, which can be measured.

ePACT **Network**—ePACT is a digital social networking platform that connects people to their entire community, providing a platform to securely share emergency information and communicate in the event of a crisis. We analyzed the emergency preparedness market to get a sense of the potential size of the market opportunity. We also analyzed ePACT's year-on-year revenue growth, user growth, and average customer size.

Analysis is helpful, but has its shortcomings. It is best suited for situations where something has already happened. To make a decision about the future in the face of uncertainty, we develop models and formulas to draw from the patterns of the past. These predictions are useful, but not infallible. There will always be uncertainty about the future, because it hasn't happened yet!

Analysis helps us take some of the guesswork out of an investment decision, but it is only one type of information. Our emotions, body, and intuition are critical for making meaningful and purposeful investment decisions in the face of uncertainty.

How Emotion Shows Up in Our Investment Decisions

Historically, investors have been encouraged to leave emotions out of investment decision making, but this is like asking investors to stop being human. Instead, I encourage you to become more aware of your emotions while investing, and understand how they influence your decisions alongside the information and inputs you get from analysis, body, and intuition.

Faced with a decision, ask yourself what you *want* to do. When you have to make a decision between what you think you should do and what you feel you want to do, your emotions generally make the final decision.

Around the time I started connecting emotions to investment decision making in 2010, my husband told me about a radio interview that he had heard with Antonio Damasio, the David Dornsife Professor of Neuroscience and Head of the Brain and Creativity Institute at the University of Southern California and Adjunct Professor at the Salk Institute. Damasio had conducted research on patients who suffered from injuries to the frontal lobe, the part of the brain that directs emotions, and his research supported what I had observed anecdotally about the importance of emotion in decision making.

Damasio gave examples of simple decision-making situations experienced by some of his patients who had lost the ability to feel emotions, such as choosing a time for an appointment or choosing a restaurant. In the former, one of his patients would deliberate logically between the merits of Tuesday or Wednesday, but struggle to actually choose between the two and make a decision. In choosing a restaurant, a patient would look at an empty restaurant and rationally analyze it, taking its emptiness as a probable bad sign that the food was not so good—but that would be followed with reasoning that the restaurant being empty meant they could get a table, so perhaps they should go there. The debate between the two choices would continue endlessly.

At the Aspen Ideas Festival in 2009, Damasio said in an interview that his patients struggled with choosing amongst options because they were missing the "lift" that comes from emotion. He makes a compelling case that it is emotion that drives people to decide something is good, bad, or something in between. His patients who experienced damage in the frontal lobe were missing the emotional impetus and therefore could not decide between one thing and another.

Damasio went on to note that our decisions can be swayed in the moment, even by small changes, because we draw from our experiences. It is not just the facts or the outcomes of an experience that influences our decisions, but also what we remember about how we felt, whether we felt good or bad about the experience.

The major conclusion drawn from Damasio's research is that the associated emotion of an outcome must be taken into consideration alongside the facts of the outcome. He believes people develop wisdom over time as a result of understanding and developing the knowledge about what our emotions tell us and what we learned from them.[1] Understanding our emotions—not ignoring them—is critical for wise, more impactful investment decision making.

---

1   "Antonio Damasio: This Time With Feeling," Aspen Ideas Festival 2009, July 4, 2009, accessed April 8, 2016, http://library.fora.tv/2009/07/04/Antonio_Damasio_This_Time_With_Feeling.

Studying the Emotional Brain

In 1994, Damasio wrote his book *Descartes' Error: Emotion, Reason, and the Human Brain,* which included research on two subjects: Phineas Gage from the 1800s, and a man named Elliott, one of Damasio's neurology patients. One of the earliest pieces of scientific research that suggested emotions are necessary for making decisions was a study of Phineas Gage, a railroad worker who, in 1848, suffered a severe injury to the frontal lobe of his brain when an iron rod pierced his head in an accident. Surprisingly, Gage survived, but he suffered from severe deficiency in practical and social decision making. According to Damasio, the case of Gage and other patients with similar frontal lobe damage presented evidence that the part of the human brain that drives emotions is critical for and inextricably connected to making decisions.[1]

Damasio wrote that after damage to the frontal lobe of the brain, basic intellect and language might not be affected; however, a person's previously learned social etiquette, and social practical and ethical rules (which is particularly interesting in an impact investing context) could be lost. Damasio's research also captured evidence of a part of the human brain that affects a person's ability to anticipate the future and plan within complex social situations and contexts, social responsibility toward one's self and others.[2] These findings, that within parts of the brain there is a strong connection amongst emotions, future-orientation, ethics, and social responsibility, have incredible impact on how investment decisions are made. Impact investing needs more than just measurement to have more effective impact. It needs emotions.

The study of Phineas Gage taught us that complex functions such as decision making and social cognition are largely dependent upon the frontal lobes. Damasio argues that emotions help us deal with uncertainty and plan for the future. Emotions point us in a direction, so that we can then put logical, rational action to good use.[3] I would add that logic, measurement,

---

1   Allison Barnes and Paul Thagard, "Emotional Decisions" (University of Waterloo, 1996), accessed April 8, 2016, http://cogsci.uwaterloo.ca/Articles/Pages/Emot.Decis.html.

2   Antonio Damasio, *Descartes' Error: Emotion, Reason, and the Human Brain* (Penguin Books, 2005), 10.

3   Damasio, *Descartes' Error*, xvii.

and analysis help narrow down the field of choices for us. But to make a decision, we need emotion to guide us.

More recent research conducted in the 1980s also supports the claim that emotions are key to decision making.

In 1985, together with Paul J. Eslinger, Damasio studied the case of his patient Elliott. He was a businessman who had a benign tumor removed from the central area of his prefrontal lobe. After the operation, Elliott experienced a series of problems and setbacks. He began to perform poorly at work, to the point of losing his job. He found himself in financial difficulty after a series of bad financial and professional decisions. He got divorced, remarried, and divorced again. Elliott was unable to get any disability support from the government at the time because he was unable to prove what his ailment was. On the face of it, there was no obvious evidence that his brain was malfunctioning. The standard neuropsychological tests at the time did not reveal anything. He scored average or above average on all the tests. Elliott's language and mathematical abilities and his memory appeared to function normally, but the problems he was experiencing showed that he was struggling to solve the problems of everyday life. Neurophysiologically, this ability arises from the cooperation between the amygdala and the frontal lobes.[1]

Damasio proposed an original theory of the mechanisms by which these structures interact. Elliott's prefrontal lobe, which is the part of the brain associated with emotions, was damaged during his operation. Damasio theorized that people whose brains demonstrated a disconnect or miscommunication between the amygdala and the frontal lobes would have problems making subtle emotional judgements of the effect and content of their actions. This flies in the face of what we've been indoctrinated with. We shouldn't be leaving emotions out of our decisions. Instead, emotions are an essential condition for being able to make rational or personal decisions in everyday life.[2] These findings are overlooked and ignored far too often. It's time we change our approach and build a greater understanding and appreciation of how emotions help us in our decision making.

---

1   The Brain from Top to Bottom, accessed April 8, 2016, www.thebrain.mcgill.ca/flash/capsules/experience_bleu04.html.

2   The Brain from Top to Bottom.

Emotions and Investment Decisions

If emotion enables and influences your decision making, it follows that it affects your ability to decide whether an investment opportunity is good, bad, or neutral. As Damasio noted, we not only remember the facts and outcomes from previous situations, we also remember whether what we felt was good or bad.

Apply that to investments and you are likely to make a decision based on the emotions you experienced as a result of a past investment decision. For example, if you invested in a first-time entrepreneur once and it felt good, you're likely to have a positive emotional reaction if presented with a similar opportunity, and therefore be inclined to make the investment again. Conversely, if your prior experience ended poorly, you're likely to be more conservative in your decision making. If you invested in a private venture previously and it didn't succeed, such that you lost your investment and felt bad about it, you're likely to be more cautious the next time you're approached with a private venture investment opportunity.

Reminders in Building Your Emotional Awareness While Making Investment Decisions

Move past the emotion of fear of investing in an opportunity. Balance this negative emotion with analysis.

Make room for the possibility of good emotions about the opportunity.

Take pause with emotions of attraction when faced with an investment opportunity. Balance these positive emotions with analysis. Weigh these emotions against caution and make a decision with your eyes open.

The analytical, logical, rational part of our brain may or may not agree with the emotional and impulsive part. When we're faced with an investment decision and uncertainty, our previous experiences and their emotional footprint will cause us to respond in ways that may blind us to the opportunities or the risks.

Reacting impulsively to an emotion may cause you to skimp on due diligence. An impulsive response to what appears to be a positive emotion, as well as a lack of awareness about a negative emotion, may cause you to ignore warning signs and end up taking undue risks. Reacting impulsively to what appears to be a negative emotion or ignoring a positive emotion, meanwhile, can cause you to pass up a good opportunity and miss out on what could be great positive change.

Some emotions you encounter in the investing experience may make you feel good. Follow them and more good feelings will follow, such as a positive investment experience with entrepreneurs you enjoy working with and who have a positive impact on the world. On the flip side, you may experience some emotions in investing that make you feel bad. Pay attention to these warning signs and you may avoid a bad investment decision, therefore yielding a good outcome. Ignore them and make an investment anyway and you could be making a bad decision. But be aware of mixed emotions, such as uneasiness about financial or operational issues with a venture. Such emotions can be warning signs, not only of potential problems with the venture, but also of bad fit or lack of readiness on your part as an investor.

If some of this sounds unclear and arbitrary to you, then I've listed some examples in the following table. Developing emotional awareness in investing is the skill of telling the difference between good and bad emotions that you should follow from those you should ignore.

This table is by no means exhaustive; rather, it is meant to be illustrative. Emotional awareness can't be developed overnight based on hard-and-fast rules. It's something you develop over time through self-awareness, self-reflection, insight, and practice.

Good Emotions: Examples	Follow Them and Make an Investment	Ignore Them and Don't Make an Investment
• Excited • Joy from working with the entrepreneur • Positive feelings about the impact the venture can have on the world • Confident about the entrepreneur and the opportunity • Proud to be investing in the entrepreneur and venture	Good outcomes	Bad outcomes (missed opportunity)
• Impulsive (would feel regret later) • Invest based on positive emotions without doing any due diligence	Bad outcomes	Good outcomes (avoid bad investment)
Bad Emotions: Examples	**Follow Them and Don't Make an Investment**	**Ignore Them and Make an Investment**
• Skepticism about the entrepreneur and the opportunity • Feeling pressured (by time or goals set) • Negative feelings about the impact the venture can have on the world • Guilt or feelings of obligation	Good outcomes	Bad outcomes (make a bad investment)
• Fearful, therefore avoid risk taking and investment opportunities altogether	Bad outcomes	Good outcomes (avoid bad investment or, in the case of not being fearful, become more open to opportunities)

People pleasing or guilt can cause us to forget our own needs as investors in our desire to try to meet an entrepreneur's needs. One investor I spoke with, Antoinette, was connected to an entrepreneur who was seeking investment for her business. She did not want to invest in the business, but she liked the entrepreneur, so she tried to introduce the person to other investors for whom she thought the opportunity might be a good fit, but that proved unsuccessful. Antoinette was committed to supporting women entrepreneurs and leaders, so out of a feeling of guilt and a sense of obligation, she invested in the entrepreneur's business. The investment was not a good one for her and she did not get her money back. Here, Antoinette went against her analysis and intuition to follow her emotions—namely, a feeling of guilt and a desire to please this entrepreneur—and it backfired on her.

Being fearful can cause us to miss opportunities because we'd rather not take the risk or don't know how to do so purposefully. This emotion often keeps people who are new to investing from taking the first step. Fear might be the response to uncertainty and risk, or fear might be the emotion resulting from feeling ill equipped to invest. Identifying the fear, determining whether there is a real risk at stake, and determining how to address the fear (by gathering more information, learning new investing skills, investing with others, or getting more practice and experience with investment amounts that won't break the bank) will help you make an appropriate decision and move forward.

Positive Emotion Can Have a Positive Impact on an Investment Decision

After meeting Catherine Dahl in 2012, I followed her progress as CEO of Beanworks Solutions, an accounting workflow automation company. I happened to bump into her at an event in 2015, and upon learning that Pique Fund had launched and that I was looking for ventures to invest in, she invited me to invest in her company. I thought she had already raised some investment and that the minimum amount was higher than what the fund was prepared to offer. Catherine told me that she had completed a seed round of investment, but that she loved what Pique Fund stood for, in particular investing in women entrepreneurs, and that even though she didn't need additional investment, she felt she could make room in order for the fund to participate. Catherine had impressed me since the first day I met her, and I had seen her mature into the CEO role and grow her business over the years, so I was excited about the opportunity to invest in her and her business. She was committed to maintaining at least a 50% female workforce in her company, something I was pleased to hear about. Her influence went beyond just her company and into her value chain. In a recent conversation with a potential partner to her business, she pointed out to the CEO that his senior management team was lacking women.

Because of the positive feelings I had about Catherine and her company, I decided to propose the investment to the committee and fellow board members. We did our due diligence and, finding no reason we should not invest, completed the deal within three weeks.

This is an investment that I feel good about. I look forward to updates from Catherine, and I'm happy to be working with her and supporting her business.

These are only a few examples of emotional reactions in investment decision making. Many other situations are possible and may arise, so you need to develop an awareness of what emotions are leading your decisions.

Greater Emotional Awareness
Can Help Us Make Better Decisions

The goal is to develop greater awareness about our emotions when faced with an investment decision, and to learn how to use that emotional information to guide our investment decisions.

Set aside the time to focus on only your emotions. The thoughts you keep in your mind should revolve around what you want to do, what you desire, and how you're feeling emotionally, not around what you should do and what you are thinking about doing. Try these exercises and practice them regularly before making an investment decision:

1. If you find yourself thinking or analyzing the situation during this exercise, pause, be patient, and redirect your concentration to your emotions.

2. Develop a meditation practice to calm your thinking brain and build your emotional awareness. Take a deep breath followed by an ohm, as is done in yoga, or try one long hum to redirect your concentration.

3. Close your eyes and take three deep breaths.

4. Concentrate on your emotions and ask yourself, "What do I want?"

5. Ask yourself what you are feeling emotionally. Take the time to pause and check in on what emotions you're feeling. Write down the first thing that comes to your mind. The point is to not overthink it.

Investor Quote: Emotions in Investing

"There was something about the teams and opportunities that spoke to my heart as much as my mind—to such an extent that I wished for them to succeed badly enough to be irrationally optimistic about their odds of success. I think it's rare for an investor to make a commitment of his or her time and capital when that emotional resonance is missing... Having the opportunity to partner with them as they build the companies they envision is a true joy. That emotional resonance leads to tight alignment with the founders' vision, goals, and preferences and a fantastic relationship, because our feelings of success are inseparable from their success in building their companies."[1]

Satya Patel, venture capital investor, ex-VP of product at Twitter, and former Google product manager

How Our Bodies Affect How We Approach Investment Risk

The physiological state of our bodies can affect our decisions. If we are hungry, thirsty, or tired, our attention shifts toward satisfying those basic needs rather than paying attention to the investment decision at hand. Before making a complex decision about investing, make sure that your basic physiological needs are met so that you can fully concentrate and be attentive to and aware of the analytical, emotional, and intuitive information available to you.

Research by former Wall Street trader turned neuroscientist John Coates indicated that higher levels of testosterone were evident in a

---

1   Satya Patel, "Chemistry and emotional resonance are key to co-investor relationships too," Venture Generated Content, November 6, 2013, accessed April 8, 2016, https://venturegeneratedcontent.com/2013/11/06/chemistry-and-emotional-resonance-are-key-to-co-investor-relationships-too/.

group of traders just before they made risky trades. As they made profitable trades, their testosterone levels went up, prompting them to make increasingly risky decisions in pursuit of ever-higher profits.

Coates also studied the role played by cortisol, the hormone released in response to stress. He found that cortisol levels were unaffected by trading losses themselves and instead found a relationship between the chemical and high variances in trading results and uncertainty in the markets. In other words, cortisol levels rose when there were big swings between the traders' profits and losses. Too much uncertainty and stress causes too much cortisol to be released, prompting fight, flight, or inhibition of action, all of which interfere with rational decision making.

The good news is that, according to Amy Cuddy, a social psychologist and associate professor at Harvard, we can proactively change our hormone levels and therefore our propensity for risk and response to stress in decision making. By adopting certain physical positions—"power poses," as she calls them—we can increase testosterone and reduce cortisol levels in our bodies. This can help you increase your appetite for risk, could cause you to make better investment decisions, and can help you cope better in stressful situations.

Awareness of Your Body in Investment Decisions

Improve your awareness of your body by observing your physical reaction to different situations that involve uncertainty or require you to make a decision. Take note of your physical state before making a decision. Are you calm or restless? Are you tired or energized?

Pay close attention to whether an investment opportunity energizes you or makes you feel like you are being depleted. Notice whether you feel physically energized to be working with a particular entrepreneur or not. A venture investment is a relationship of give and take. Too much give and you can feel drained of your energy. An exciting venture investment opportunity is one that you can physically feel good about.

Over time, observe the patterns of physical sensations in your body when faced with different daily decisions. For example, when I'm feeling stressed or anxious about a decision, I feel a physical sensation in my upper arms, as if cold water is rushing through my veins or under my skin. When a situation is good or I receive positive information about something, I get tingles down the back of neck and across my upper back. Take your increased awareness of your own body's patterns in daily situations and apply it to investment decision-making situations to help you determine whether an opportunity is favorable for you or not.

When faced with a decision that requires risk taking, adopt a power pose, as suggested by Amy Cuddy. Power poses have the effect of temporarily increasing testosterone levels in your body, preparing you for greater risk taking, if that is what you want to do.

Using Intuition to Make Decisions in the Face of Investment Uncertainty

We need intuition for those big leaps of faith that investing sometimes requires. Intuition is difficult to put a finger on. It is often something that neither emotions nor logic can explain. In fact, it typically flies in the face of rational thinking. Intuition, when we tap into it, supports our decision to proceed when we might otherwise be fearful and even when the odds are stacked against us. Intuition helps us access our deeper knowledge, which is otherwise buried under over-calculation and overanalysis. Intuition is the warning feeling we get when something is presented to us and, although it looks and feels pleasant, deep down we know or sense it is not.

Intuition guides you in a particular direction and is critical for making decisions about the unknown, uncertain future. Trend analysis, pattern recognition, extrapolation, and other predictive models use past data to predict an investment's future outcomes, but we have to qualify these predictions with the caution that past performance is not an infallible predictor of future investment results. There is no such thing as a future fact.

Analysis as an information input into our investment decision making about the future is limited because you cannot analyze something that has not yet happened. Even emotions are biased by past experiences. How do you feel something that hasn't happened yet? Instinct is about survival and avoiding known dangers. Instinct is physiological, and our physiology adapts to dangers we have experienced. But that also relies on past experience.

Analysis and emotion help narrow the field in our due diligence and rule out alternatives. Instincts keep us alive and safe from danger. But for complex decisions about the uncertain future where other unknown factors could affect outcomes, like investments, we need some other input to guide our decisions—and that information comes from intuition.

Intuition is the only forward-looking input. It allows us to fill in gaps in information about future personal responses to outcomes. It is particularly useful in choosing partners, places to live, and anything relationship-oriented, whether with ourselves or others. Intuition helps mediate between competing goals and desires and enables us to make a choice that optimizes our decision.

Humans have a tendency to make intuitive and subjective matters analytical. We are obsessed with measurement and comparison. Why not trust intuition?

While there is research supporting the idea that emotions play a big role in decision making, discernment, and judgment, intuition is a less studied input. Perhaps there is something in the brain that enables us to suspend disbelief, ignore emotions that might impede us (like fear), or ignore immediate gratification in lieu of long-term benefit. The challenge with conducting research on intuition is that most people don't know to test for it until long after the intuitive decision has been made and hindsight tells them it was good. I (intuitively) know it exists, because how else do we imagine the unimaginable? How else do we create things that have not been done before? Why believe the Earth is round when everyone else "knows" it is flat? Intuition guides us to explore these things further.

Actively Engaging Intuition in Investment Decision Making

Successful investors will credit their intuition, although they will not spend a lot of time talking about it. This is because intuition does not originate from our rational and logical brain, which makes it hard to explain it. But we all have the ability to access our intuition and consciously engage it in our investment decision-making processes.

I have trusted my intuition in making decisions about my career path, my partner, relocation, and who to work with. Analysis about a situation helps me make an objective assessment, emotions draw me to what I know or away from what I fear, and intuition leads me toward the grand opportunities I do not yet have any evidence of. How could I possibly have known all there is to know about a career path in investment banking before entering that industry? How could I have known about my husband before we married, or about London or Vancouver before I relocated halfway around the world?

I apply integrated decision making to many areas of my life, but particularly to investing, because it is inherently a future-oriented activity. How can I know all there is to know about the entrepreneurs and ventures I'm considering investing in? I can analyze the opportunity and the entrepreneurs and be aware of how I feel about them, but it's my intuition that fills in the gaps and guides me toward the future outcomes I seek.

Try it out for yourself. Look back on a big, life-changing decision you made that involved your relationship with yourself or others and reflect on what drove your decision. Did it require a lot of analysis? Did your emotions guide you? Was your survival instinct involved? Or was it something else? How did you respond to the outcome of that decision? Did the numbers stack up afterward? Did you feel elated or disappointed?

Now try this exercise in relation to a current decision you face. Start by clearing your mind. Meditation or a walk through a natural environment helps. Reflect on what your analytical brain is thinking, what your emotions are sensing, and what your body is feeling, and then ask what your intuition tells you. Your decisions will be optimized when all four of these things are in sync. We can make decisions when all four are not in sync, but if you are aware of which of them is leading the decision—be it analysis, emotion, body, or intuition—you are less likely to be surprised by the outcome.

The biggest challenge we face at the moment are the outcomes resulting from decisions that were over-weighted by analysis. These outcomes make sense analytically (aka, the numbers stack up), but there is something dissatisfying and not sufficiently nurturing about them. This is the problem in business, and in the investment sector in particular. Investment decisions are too analytical. They do not encompass enough emotion or intuition. The solution is not a bifurcation of investments into "conventional" investments and impact or socially responsible investing; what we actually need is integrated investing—an integration of information from analysis, emotion, body, and intuition into our investment decisions. That integration will lead to outcomes that satisfy our analytical, emotional, physical, and intuitive needs and enable economic viability, prosperity, and the thriving lives and communities we all seek.

Integrating Analysis, Emotion, Body, and Intuition into Investment Decisions

Before making an investment decision, ask yourself the following questions:

- What do I think I should do?
- What do I want to do?
- What signals is my body giving me?
- What would I intuitively do?

The first question engages your analytical brain, and your response is based on the analysis you've performed. The second is about your emotions and the direction they are guiding you in. The third asks you to pay attention to the state of your body and the physical sensations you might be experiencing. The fourth taps into your intuition. To best answer this question calling upon your intuition, I highly recommend you do whatever practice you've found helps you engage your intuition, be it meditation, going for a walk, relaxing, or even just closing your eyes.

These four questions are good to keep in mind and to practice if you face the opportunity to do some integrated investment decision making—that is, integrating analysis, emotion, body, and intuition into your investment decision making. Optimal investment decisions result when you have done your analysis and due diligence, when you are aware of your emotional reaction and pay attention to how emotions are guiding your decisions, when you are aware of the physical signals your body is giving you, and when you are aware of your intuition and how it guides your decisions in the face of uncertainty.

This approach is an important cornerstone for you on your journey toward integrated investing.

6

MINDSETS

I FIRST NOTICED THE importance of mindsets in investing shortly after I transitioned from investment banking to impact investing, and I began to think of investments as relationships rather than as transactions. This could have been in part because my transition involved shifting from working with faceless investment products to working directly with entrepreneurs trying to make a positive difference in the world with their ventures. My relationship lens—or relationship mindset—fit with the fact that I was working closely with people again, which reminded me that investing activities, at the end of the day, are all about people. Even the investment products of my banking days were about people (somewhere at the other end of a long, opaque transaction line), but that industry seemed to have forgotten about that and had distanced itself from the people it was affecting. This difference has been one of the most noticeable contrasts between my work as an investment banker in the mid-2000s and my work in the impact investing industry, where I am now. Whereas banking activities were depersonalized and data-driven, in impact investing we pay far greater attention to the people involved and the impact our actions have on people, both directly and indirectly.

At the start of 2013, I began to notice how the outcomes of my decisions varied depending on what mindset I was in at the time. Sometimes I was too much in a mindset of serving others and not focused enough on exchange. In one situation, I didn't get what I needed out of a business relationship, paid more money than I could afford at the time, and focused too much on helping her as opposed to an arrangement where we both could get what we needed. When I experience a dip in cash flow, revenues, or investment returns, or if an entrepreneur conveys poorer-than-expected results in their business, the impulse is for a scarcity mindset to creep in, which makes decision making focus on the short-term. I have become aware of how an exchange and abundance mindset can help me make decisions that are more beneficial to me and to people I do business with. As a result of these experiences and self-reflection, I now make an effort to be cognizant of what mindset I'm in before making a major financial decision.

After reflecting on different decision-making experiences, I made note of the mindsets I was in at the time and came up with the six most critical mindset groups for me. The way you frame a situation and the way you look at the world can strongly influence your decisions. Mindsets are like a muscle you need to train and flex. They are not static. You need to practice to maintain the mindsets that are most conducive to confident and positive investment decision making.

In this chapter, I will discuss the six mindset groups I feel are most important. I've divided them into three categories.

- Mindsets that affect your perception about resources and risk:
  - Abundance and scarcity
  - Curiosity and fear

- Mindsets that influence how you relate to and interact with others:
  - Exchange, self-interest, and serving others
  - Relationship and transaction

- Mindsets that affect your frame of mind about results:
  - Future potential and past performance
  - Resources and money

Abundance and Scarcity

Have you ever noticed how your decision-making style changes when you're thinking on an empty stomach versus when you've just had a satisfying meal? When you're hungry, not only does your physiological drive to search for food influence your decisions and direction, it can also conjure a sense of scarcity. Feeling satiated, in contrast, gives a sense of abundance—at least in the short term—while you relish the meal you just had.

The abundance and scarcity mindsets reflect these feelings. They are perspectives about resources, things, feelings, or states of being that you have or that you want to be present in your life.

An abundance mindset goes beyond the physical and the physiological. It is a perception. It is how your brain thinks about what you are full of or what is present in your life. It is the thought that you have and will have all the resources, financial and non-financial, that you need. With an abundance mindset, you approach investing with the feeling that you are abundant in the time, money, experience, and expertise required to make a deal.

An abundance mindset in investing is associated with a feeling of creating more of something as a result of your investment decision—more resources, more investing experience, and more impact. This mindset means you can serve your own self-interest and serve others simultaneously.

Abundance Mindset	Scarcity Mindset
Expect high performance and high impact	Expect failure
Investment with a return and impact	Hoard assets
There is more where that came from	This is all that I have, that I'll ever have
Build trust	Lack trust
I have enough to meet my needs and can invest in others	There isn't enough to be shared
Prioritize resources to enable investment	Not enough resources to invest

A scarcity mindset is the perspective that there are not enough resources to go around. It breeds the attitude that "if I invest this and lose it, there's no more where it came from." Scarcity breeds feelings and attitudes of risk aversion.

In the context of investing, an abundance mindset can mean anything from literally feeling abundant enough in money that you can make an investment (you have enough money that you can allocate some of it toward investing in impactful ventures), or it can mean feeling abundant enough in time and energy that you're willing to evaluate new opportunities and advise entrepreneurs that you have invested in. You may need to feel abundant in other things, such as ideas, creativity, or knowledge, to feel there are no barriers to you making an investment.

When I am in a scarcity mindset, in particular regarding money, I am more reluctant to invest. I scrutinize opportunities more closely, and I demand more from my investments. If I'm in a scarcity mindset about time, I won't spend the time that is needed to properly evaluate an entrepreneur and a venture, nor will I spend the time needed to carry out due diligence. If I feel I don't have enough time to do the due diligence, I won't invest.

With an abundance mindset, if an investment doesn't turn out the way I expected—or worse yet, if it fails—I still know I have gained something from the experience, and that the investment will open a door or prepare me for another opportunity around the corner.

An abundance mindset in the entrepreneurs I invest in means they're looking for business opportunities where abundance lies. A scarcity mindset could mean they operate their ventures in a miserly way that stifles growth and opportunity. Worse yet, they may believe there are not enough resources to go around, possibly leading to staff or suppliers being underpaid to maintain margins and profit. A scarcity mindset can lead to poor decision making and situations of inequity.

How to Develop an Abundance Mindset
To develop an abundance mindset, begin with the belief that there are more than enough resources to go around. Develop a mindfulness practice that enables you to embrace and embody this belief. A mindfulness

practice might include meditation or self-affirmation on the concept of abundant resources.

To get grounded in an abundance mindset, think about past situations when you have experienced or had a feeling of abundance. What did those situations look and feel like? What were their characteristics? Imagine yourself in those situations to bring yourself back into an abundance mindset.

Curiosity and Fear

My mindset about unknown and uncertain situations is rooted in curiosity. I am also the sort of person to be curious about what lies around the corner.

In 2012, a young woman at a networking event I attended, who was just beginning her career, shared with me her desire to move abroad. Although something was clearly driving her to explore traveling and working in a different culture and environment, she was also a bit scared of the change that would mean. I mentioned to her that I had lived in the UK for twelve years and made a few moves in my career amidst uncertainty, but fear had never held me back. The young woman asked me what had enabled me to make the move without fear, and I told her that my curiosity about different cities, new roles, and meeting new people had excited and energized me in instances where the environment, situation, or outcomes were unknown. She was inspired by my story and promised to keep it in mind when making her decision.

After that conversation, I realized that I apply that same curiosity to investing. I am genuinely curious about what an investment from Pique Fund or me personally can do to support an emerging leader and business. What lies around the corner if I give this entrepreneur and venture a chance?

The curiosity and fear mindsets are perspectives on risk and how to approach uncertainty and the unknown.

Curiosity is defined as a strong desire to know or learn something. A curiosity mindset prompts inquiry, inquisitiveness, and learning. It can help propel you forward in the face of uncertainty.

In investing, be curious about an entrepreneur and their venture. Adopt a curiosity mindset and be inquisitive about what the entrepreneur and their team can accomplish. Be curious about how a venture's product or service can address a problem. Be curious about how an investment opportunity and decision might turn out.

A curiosity mindset encourages you to learn and find out more through the experience of investing in an opportunity and letting the uncertain future unfold in front of you.

A fear mindset, on the other hand, can keep you from moving forward. Fear encourages the status quo and avoids change. Being fearful about investing in a venture keeps you from taking a step forward to learn more about the opportunity. Rather than inspiring you to ask questions or seek help, a fear mindset blocks off the opportunity.

Curiosity Mindset	Fear Mindset
What if?	That's okay
Embraces change	Maintains status quo
Desire to explore and discover	Preference for staying where you are
Develops a hypothesis and tests it	Requires someone else to have proven it
Aware of intuition, follows intuition	Dependent solely upon analysis and reason

To develop a curiosity mindset, focus on asking questions rather than knowing the answers. Be inquisitive.

Imagine yourself as someone that personifies curiosity, like explorers, adventure travelers, detectives, and astronauts. Imagine investing as an expedition you're leading, or that the opportunity you're considering is like a city you're about to discover. Do detective work on the entrepreneur and venture not knowing how the case will unfold. Imagine investing in a venture as exploring space and new frontiers.

Children are also great role models for curiosity. Try looking at your investment opportunities through the eyes of a child experiencing their surroundings for the first time. Children are naturally curious, with hardly any bounds.

Keep an open mind and remove any limitations you may be placing on your investment decisions. An open mind is a curious mind.

Self-Interest, Serving Others, and Exchange

Capitalism is rooted in the idea that serving self-interest is the biggest, most effective economic motivator in society. Big business has been built on Keynesian economic principles that worship the motivational power of self-interest.

When I started focusing on impact investing in 2010, a lot of my colleagues in the social enterprise and not-for-profit sectors told me how the focus and mission of their business activities should be about serving others—about being "others-interested." Debates ensued about how people are inherently selfish, even when performing seemingly selfless acts for others. We feel good about helping other people, and that got me thinking. Where we focus our interest is not binary. It is not a mutually exclusive competition between serving self or serving others; the focus is inclusive. In my own experience, the feeling of a fair exchange is what truly leaves me feeling that I met my own self-interest and served others while doing so.

A self-interest mindset places your own needs ahead of anyone else's. If self-interest is the top thing on your mind when you're faced with a number of investment choices, you'll make decisions that serve you and your interests first. In investing, this means concentrating on "What's in it for me?" However, too much of a focus on yourself will make it challenging to part with your money, your time, and your energy. Investing inherently involves other people, in particular the entrepreneurs at the helm of the ventures you're investing in. So the self-interest mindset must also be balanced with other mindsets.

A serving others mindset influences you to make decisions that put others' needs ahead of your own. It is a mindset of generosity and giving to others. With it, you might find yourself compromising or even sacrificing the satisfaction of your own needs and interests in order to meet the needs of others, which can leave you drained of your financial resources and feeling mentally exhausted as well. So the mindset of serving others must be balanced with self-interest.

The balance between self-interest and serving others is what I call an exchange mindset. With it, you're going to choose the investment opportunity where there is the best exchange of value. That is, you gain from what the opportunity can give you (financial benefit, kudos, experience, connections to others in the venture's network), and the venture gains from what you are giving (financial resources, expertise, advice, and connections).

Exchange Mindset	Self-Interest Mindset	Serving Others Mindset
Us and them, together	Me	Them
Give and take	Take	Give
Community	Selfish	Selfless
Collaborative	Competitive	Charitable
Fair	Greed	Sacrifice

The Ultimatum Game

In the Ultimatum Game, invented by German sociologist Werner Güth in the early 1980s, you receive a fixed amount of money, say, ten dollars, to share with a stranger according to some rules. You must offer the stranger a proportion of the money. If the stranger accepts your offer, you and the stranger leave the game with the agreed amounts. If the stranger rejects your offer, you get the ten dollars back and you both leave with nothing. The roles can be reversed. If you were offered ten dollars from a stranger under the same rules, which offers would you accept and or reject? Researchers have studied the outcomes of this game over the past thirty years, and offers are typically at least 30%, with the most common offer by proposers being 50%. Responders usually reject anything less than 30%. In his book *Basic Instincts: Human Nature and the New Economics*, Pete Lunn believes the explanation for this behavior is that our instincts associated with fairness are stronger and outweigh our selfish emotions for money.[1]

---

1   Pete Lunn, *Basic Instincts: Human Nature and the New Economics* (London, Marshall Cavendish Business, 2010), 104.

Why is an Exchange Mindset Recommended for Investing?

An exchange mindset has fairness at its heart and sets the stage for a more successful investment relationship. There will be fewer hard feelings, any feelings of unfairness will be less likely, and no one will try to gain an advantage and cheat the other person later on.

The exchange mindset in investing means both investor and entrepreneur are getting their needs met. Perhaps both have to compromise in some way for an agreement to be reached, but because the investment relationship is rooted in the belief that the investor is getting something in exchange for something else and the entrepreneur is gaining, also in exchange, the foundation is set for a relationship based on trust, open communication, and mutual success for both parties.

How to Develop an Exchange Mindset

To develop an exchange mindset, start with the abundance mindset and trust that there are enough resources to go around to meet your interests and to serve others. Don't just ask yourself, "What's in it for me?" Also ask, "What's in it for them?" Head into an investment relationship with the belief that the relationship holds value for both of you.

Keep in mind that, more often than not, it is not a like-for-like exchange. Know what is of value to you and what is of value to the entrepreneur and their business, and work toward a give-and-take exchange.

Keep the following in mind:

- As an investor, if I take something from you, the entrepreneur, it is fair for me to give you something in exchange.
- As an investor, if I give something to you, the entrepreneur, it is fair to receive something in exchange.

Relationship and Transaction

I'm lucky to be working in a field where all the investment activities I've been involved in have included direct communication with the entrepreneurs and business leaders who owned the companies in which I was considering investing. In my career, I've exclusively worked in what is called the alternative investment field, which means I make private investments, be it in equity, debt, or impact venture capital. The approach that my colleagues and I have taken in the field of impact investing is to treat our interactions with entrepreneurs and their companies as investment relationships, not just as financial transactions.

The efficient packaging up of investment opportunities into investment products has become more opaque over time. People understand their investments less and as a result, have become less engaged and less involved in the direction of their investment activities and decisions. People are becoming disgruntled and dissatisfied with the financial advisors that manage their investments for them, or unhappy about the companies in which their money is being invested. Companies seem to be less accountable for their actions, and as investors, we increasingly feel there is little we can do to change things. But we can change things with a relationship mindset.

A relationship mindset is about connection between people, and it implies something longer-term and enduring. Adopting a relationship mindset about investing reminds you that it is about people—it humanizes the investing experience. This approach makes investing less about transacting and takes some of the emphasis off money. There is a close connection between the relationship mindset and the exchange mindset. Many of the underlying principles are the same; they both encourage and rely upon on trust, transparency, and open communication.

A transaction mindset, on the other hand, focuses on the buying and selling of a product or service. It turns investing into a product and encourages you to focus on the exchange of money. The transaction mindset implies something short-term and fleeting.

A transaction mindset dehumanizes our interactions in investing because it places emphasis on an exchange of goods or services and money. It is because of this mindset that investing has become increasingly impersonal over the years.

If you can embrace the idea that investing is, at the end of the day, all about people by developing a relationship mindset, you will find yourself investing in a different way, and will experience a greater sense of success.

Relationship Mindset	Transaction Mindset
Focus on people	Focus on products
Build over time, long	Immediacy, fleeting
Requires high trust	Characterized by low trust
Focus on connection and fit	Focus on buying and selling
Experiential	Process

Investing in a private venture is about the entrepreneur, their team, and the relationship they have with you, the investor. The people involved in a venture are critical to the success of your investment. This can sometimes be taken for granted with a transaction mindset. If you approach venture investing with only a transaction mindset, you will end up missing information and nuances about the entrepreneur and the venture, and that can contribute to the investment's failure. A relationship mindset reminds you to engage with and evaluate an investment opportunity as you would engage with and evaluate people in a relationship context. Skills and qualities that we associate with relationships—trust, empathy, and communication, for example—will be useful to you in your investment decision making. A relationship mindset reminds you to take time to get to know the venture and the people involved.

Why a Relationship Mindset is Important to Investing

A relationship mindset is useful in investing because it helps you focus on forming a good relationship with the CEOs and management teams in which you are investing. Good relationships encourage CEOs and management teams to have greater transparency with their investors, and to engage in better governance.

It sets the stage for healthier, more productive conversations between investors and management teams, in particular in times of trouble or if they are facing a challenge. Conversely, a relationship mindset is also important when things are going smoothly, as it creates an environment for open dialogue and communication, which can lead to the creation of more opportunities. It helps investors and management teams be less confrontational and adversarial, and more successful.

How to Get into a Relationship Mindset

Developing a relationship mindset starts with a focus on people. At the end of the day, when we speak of the potential of a company, we primarily mean that of the leadership team and staff—their potential to work together to achieve something great.

To develop a future potential mindset, practice the following:

- Focus on people.
- Focus on mutual trust and respect.
- Contemplate transparency and open communication.
- Think of your investment activities as interpersonal and about connection.
- Care about who you are interacting with—is this someone you want to go through good and bad times with?

Mindsets Matter: Moving Forward with Micro-Business Lending

Joy Anderson, President of Criterion Institute and one of my advisors, was working with senior leaders of a church congregation. They were discussing establishing a micro-business loan fund within the church to fund members who were planning to start new businesses. The subject was a $500 starter loan. "What if they steal the money?" one of the church leaders asked. Joy highlighted that the church leaders would have the opportunity to establish relationships with members who borrowed the money that would be based on trust and mutual benefit. "You mean, we can actually talk to our members?" they asked with delight.

This, to me, is an illustration of an opportunity to engage mindsets of curiosity, abundance, and relationship. A curiosity mindset enables the church leaders to be open to the possibilities and be curious about how a micro-business loan could benefit her congregation. An abundance mindset would encourage them to believe that there were enough resources to go around and that lending money to a congregation member could actually reap more through the growth of a new small business. The most critical shift in mindset, however, is to one of relationship. A micro-business loan is more than just the transfer and transaction of money. It is an extension of the existing relationships they have with their congregation members, creating a sense of accountability deeply rooted in mutual trust and benefit.

Although becoming micro-lenders was new territory for the church leaders, their skill, experience, and strength in relationship-building with their congregation was a solid foundation on which to build lending relationships.

Future Potential and Past Performance

I first took notice of this mindset when I was working in the impact investing team of a large financial institution. I was evaluating an opportunity to provide a loan to a company and assessing its ability to meet the obligations of the loan in the future. There was so much uncertainty and potential for change associated with the company that it was more like an investment opportunity than a lending opportunity. My boss at the time asked me for financial ratios and wanted more analysis of the company's past performance. I felt agitated by the request, which is a bit strange considering my accounting and banking background. I felt that the financial ratios and analysis of the company's past performance wasn't going to tell me what I needed to know about the company's potential.

Conventional investment methodologies use past performance to try to predict the future, assuming that past patterns and trends will continue, but that's where our assumptions can fail us. Faced with uncertainty and change, there is a big chance that old patterns and trends won't continue. As much as we might think it is, past performance is no indicator of the future performance or potential of a company.

On this job I realized I did not have the right investment methodology to make a satisfactory impact investing decision and appease my boss. I realized that I needed to adopt a future potential mindset as opposed to a past performance mindset.

Investing outcomes are future-oriented. Investors spend a lot of time analyzing the past performance of the entrepreneur, the sector or industry, or the venture they are considering investing in if they have some operating history. Past performance tells you important information about where the entrepreneur and venture have come from and what their journey has been. However, this limits your scope, as it doesn't tell you what you need to know about the future.

Looking at past performance doesn't make it any easier to know what will happen in the future. A venture could continue performing the way it always has, or it could perform well for a while and then run into trouble. Our objectives for ventures more likely center around them growing and doing something different—perhaps expanding into new markets or launching new products and services. Repeating the past, even if past performance was good, is not what we're looking for as venture investors. Past performance is no guarantee of future performance, and certainly isn't an indicator of future potential.

A future potential mindset focuses more on what could be with an investment opportunity than on what has already been done. It goes hand in hand with the curiosity mindset, and shares the same elements of discovery and exploration. Future potential evokes the unlocking of abilities of the entrepreneur and venture opportunities that were not previously visible.

Future Potential Mindset	Past Performance Mindset
What could be	What has been
Looking forward	Looking back
Financial projections	Historical financial statements
Guesswork, hypothesis, assumptions	Knowledge, facts, data
Intuition	Analysis
Focus on people, team, and communication amongst them	Focus on metrics, accounting, and the company's financial results

How to Apply Future Potential Mindset to Investing

Investing is inherently a future-oriented activity. A future potential mindset helps you broaden your mind and focus on outcomes. It enables you to focus on an entrepreneur's vision and the future market opportunity of a venture. Giving an entrepreneur and their venture a chance by believing in and investing in their potential is the beginning of what could be a self-fulfilling prophecy.

In evaluating an entrepreneur's potential, look at how they handle feedback and change. Are they responsive to change, or do they ignore it? Do they demonstrate judgment and balance in adopting feedback or standing their ground at different times?

How they've dealt with past situations, not their performance in them, can give some indication of future potential. In other words, an entrepreneur's vision and how the entrepreneur makes decisions is a better indication of their potential than past performance ever could be.

The future potential mindset can also be applied to your evaluation of market opportunities. With it, you could consider how potential customers of the company you are evaluating might make decisions to purchase products and services down the line.

How to Develop a Future Potential Mindset

Similar to a relationship mindset, developing a future potential mindset starts with a focus on people. At the end of the day, when we speak of future potential of a company, we primarily mean that of the leadership team and the staff, and how they will interact and relate to each other to achieve something great together.

Practice the following to develop a future potential mindset:

- Focus on a person's strengths rather than their weaknesses (in particular, the potential strengths in a person that may require further support and development).

- Give people the benefit of the doubt where possible.

- Ask people about their dreams and vision of the future to help you develop a future-orientation; do they have vision, determination, drive, a propensity to learn, and a propensity for risk and change?

- Imagine what is possible.

- Take the limits off.

- Embrace "what if."

- Engage your intuition.

- Develop your future-orientation by reading future-oriented science fiction and social fiction.

Resources and Money

Just the other day, a relative asked me why the world revolves around money. This question prompted a conversation about the purpose of money, and other family members chimed in. We talked about the power that money represents, and another relative noted that what we were really talking about were values and what we actually need to sustain ourselves.

Money's primary role is as a means of exchange. Yet the prevailing money mindset would have us believe that it is the be all and end all or that it sustains us. But that isn't true. We can't eat money if we're hungry, or drink it if we're thirsty. Money won't keep us warm and protect us from the elements. We can only exchange it for the essential resources we need to sustain ourselves.

Money is a concept that was created so that we could more easily exchange our time spent and the resources we owned for other things we needed. So money is a means, not an end. But when we adopt a money mindset, we make it the end goal.

Some people use money as an essential resource of expression, as if the numbers on their paychecks or bank accounts actually tell other people something meaningful about them. Here again, the money mindset disconnects us from the essential resources we need.

As investment bankers, my colleagues and I worked with a lot of money every day. We were also paid handsomely; on personal levels we all had access to quite a lot of money. But we were always seeking something more. Some boasted about the extravagant holidays or new homes their money could afford. Some of us talked about working in investment banking for a couple of years, just until we earned enough money to quit and do what we really wanted to do. In both cases, we were all engaged in a chase for more money. This mindset distracts many of us from what is really important to us, what we actually want and need.

The financial crisis and credit crunch in 2007 and 2008 demonstrated that money is not all it was cracked up to be. It is fleeting. Banks, governments, and people made decisions with money irresponsibly. This caused me to rethink the money mindset. I began to focus more on the people I wanted to spend time with, the things I wanted to spend more time doing, and the resources I actually wanted and needed. I traveled and stayed with faraway friends who were not part of the investment banking industry. I reconnected with ways of life that were not as caught up in the money mindset as I had been in investment banking. I spent time with my family. I took up new hobbies and reacquainted myself with old ones. I was creative with my resources. All of this was leading me to develop a new mindset.

A resources mindset connects us to the things we actually need to sustain ourselves in life, thrive, and be happy.

Resources Mindset	Money Mindset
What we really need are essential resources for sustenance, expression, connection, managing change, making decisions, and as a means of exchange	Money sustains us
Money as a means of exchange	Money as an end goal
Focus on multiple stakeholders, including shareholders, customers, employees, partners, suppliers, the planet, and the community	Focus on shareholders
Focus on optimizing essential resources for stakeholders	Focus on maximizing profits for shareholders

Why a Resources Mindset Is Important to Investing

A resources mindset in investing helps integrated investors focus on a set of returns and outcomes that are broader than just a focus on profits and money. It makes investing about more than just money. Investing becomes about ensuring people get access to the essential resources they need.

Whereas a money mindset is associated with the outdated and incomplete idea of maximizing profits for shareholders, a resources mindset concentrates investors' efforts on optimizing essential resources for all stakeholders impacted by a business. By "stakeholders," I mean shareholders, customers, employees, partners, suppliers, communities, and the planet.

How to Develop a Resources Mindset

Developing a resources mindset requires thinking differently about money and the things you need to survive, thrive, and be happy. Reviewing the essential resources mentioned in Chapter 1 is helpful. Here are some things to keep in mind to help you toward a resources mindset:

- Move past money and focus more on the essential resources—on what money can buy.
- Think of money as a means of exchange, not an end unto itself.
- Think about what you need. Start by asking, "What does money buy me that I need?"
- Think about what things or resources you need every day rather than thinking about the money you need to buy them.

Summary

In this chapter, we have explored three categories of mindsets, and in each, two groups of mindsets:

- Mindsets that affect your perception about resources and risk:
  - Abundance and scarcity
  - Curiosity and fear

- Mindsets that influence your outlook on how to relate to and interact with others:
  - Exchange, self-interest, and serving others
  - Relationship and transaction

- Mindsets that affect your frame of mind about results, which includes:
  - Future potential and past performance
  - Resources and money

The mindsets of abundance, curiosity, exchange, relationship, future potential, and resources help integrated investors achieve more impact in their investing.

7

INTEGRATED INVESTING
TOOLKIT

I STARTED DEVELOPING INTEGRATED investing with two big questions in mind. First, how do we make investment decisions differently to move investment dollars in a more purposeful way? Second, why isn't the investor community more diverse?

Traditional investment methods and evaluation tools have been around for decades without challenge. These methods and tools are highly quantitative and assume that a number or a ratio can measure everything important. Formulas and models such as net present value, internal rate of return, return on investment, and alpha, beta, and sharpe ratios from traditional investing are rooted in old number and mathematical systems, accounting principles, and investment models that are based on incomplete assumptions about people, their wants in life, and their behaviors. Traditional investment methods and evaluation tools are often based on probabilities, averages, and generalities that don't always hold true as people, communities, and economies change.

Few have stopped to question whether these methods and tools are actually effective. Do they really help us achieve all of our investment goals and desires? In my opinion, no—and the credit crunch and financial crisis of 2007-8 should be indication enough that those methods are flawed and outdated.

I was first exposed to the impact investing space in 2009, and at that time I was already perplexed that colleagues in the industry were talking about striving for both financial and positive social outcomes from their investing, yet the methods they used were basically variations of the same thing my investment banking colleagues in the traditional markets used. Performance measurement models that have been introduced into impact investing, such as social return on investment, attempt to place a number on social impact. Social return on investment relies on the same formula as traditional investing, and it uses outdated benchmarks for the inputs into the formula. How should childcare be valued, what is the cost of educating someone, what is the environmental cost of transportation alternatives? These are used rather than challenging old assumptions. Even more basic still, accounting ratios and traditional measures of profitability and growth are used to evaluate impact investing opportunities.

We needed to do things differently. With this in mind, I set out to develop a set of investment methods and tools that would reflect our current situation and the blended future outcomes we aspire to.

In earlier chapters, I talked about mindsets and different investment perspectives that lay the foundation for integrated investing. This chapter will set out the practical tips and tools that you can apply and enact in your investment activities to help you identify and evaluate impactful investment opportunities. Some traditional tools and practices that have been used in some form for decades, such as due diligence and scenario analysis, remain fundamental and useful. Some of what we will discuss are contemporary tools that emerged in the 2000s for entrepreneurs building new ventures, and which I have adapted for use by investors evaluating opportunities because they are just as useful from an investor perspective; understanding how entrepreneurs are thinking and how new businesses are being developed, after all, is critical to your investing activities. Last and most important, I will share impact evaluation tools. These are key to differentiating impactful investment opportunities from traditional ones.

Start with What You Know

When you are new to investing in private ventures with impact or are feeling like you need to gain more experience, start with what you know. Knowledge provides you with a starting point for your investment choices.

For example, if you were to try to invest in a private venture in the renewable energy industry, but you knew nothing about renewable and alternative energy, you would have to expend extra time and energy to learn the key features of that industry. You would be starting at a disadvantage compared to an investor already well versed in the sector.

You can take one step toward lowering your risk by investing in a field of business or industry you know, in a venture related to a subject area that you've learned in formal education or through the school of life, in something you're interested in and have spent time being involved in, or alongside people you know and trust who are knowledgeable about an industry or business.

You Know Your Work

Perhaps you're an experienced entrepreneur who's been running your own business for the last ten years. Or maybe you're a working professional with years of experience that you would love to share with others. Maybe your work experience has been in the same industry throughout your career, or maybe you have moved around and experimented in different fields, adding to your expertise with every move. In the context of figuring out what you know so that you can direct your investing activities in that direction, your work is your starting point.

Know Where Your Work and Interests Intersect

I met a man who was a successful business development and sales executive who had launched a technology business in the 1990s in Europe. He later went on to lead sales and marketing for a technology company in the health and wellness industry, and, after that, worked for a technology company focused on the real estate sector. He had tried his hand before in private investing, but his previous angel investments had been unsuccessful. In this second attempt, he began by concentrating on private ventures in a field in which he had worked before: the intersection of technology and health and wellness, as well as real estate related technology startups. He advised a crowdfunding platform that focused on helping people meet the cost of paying for exceptional medical procedures or for medical bills arising from an accident or unexpected illness. He also invested in a technology startup that served the real estate industry and was able to help them make important industry connections (which eventually led to a successful acquisition). In his renewed attempt at angel investing, this investor knew to focus on what he knew.

To provide you with some direction and a jumping-off point from your current profession, the table on the following page highlights some of the roles in investing you can explore depending upon what industry or career role you have been in. This table is not comprehensive, but hopefully it will give you an idea of what is possible.

Here are some questions you can ask yourself to help you connect with potential ventures and investment opportunities:

- What changes are happening in my industry and with my work?
- What challenges does my industry face that I would like to see addressed?
- What positive changes, solutions, or innovations would I like to see happen in my industry?

Look for entrepreneurs and ventures that are at the forefront of such changes or are developing the kind of solutions you would like to see.

Your industry	The role that you might occupy in your industry	Related industries, ventures, or your role in investing in a new venture
Medical and health care	Doctor, dentist, nurse, paramedic, health care professional (alternative, mental health, physical health and disabilities)	Medical technology, ventures focused on health care service delivery (could include how medical information is shared, medical training, and new forms of service delivery and systems)
Media	Publisher, editor, writer, journalist, film producer, music producer, director	Digital and new models of publishing, creative content, technology-enabled media platforms, training, distribution, media sharing
Finance	Accountant, finance director, chief financial officer, banker, financial advisor	Fintech (financial technology), how financial information is shared and distributed, advising on the finance functions of new ventures (CFO support)
Marketing, advertising, communications, and community	Marketing professional, sales professional, communications professional, publicist, community manager, CSR professional, advertising agent, media buyer	New marketing channels, platforms for marketing products and services, advising on marketing and communications functions of new ventures
Management consulting	Management consultant, business consultant or advisor	New business models, advising on business strategy, operations, and product strategy for new ventures
Design, development, and innovation	Designer, developer, researcher	How design talent is accessed, new models, how design and tech development information is shared and distributed, advising on design and development for new ventures

You Know Your Interests

What are you passionate about? What do you invest a lot of your spare time in? Your personal interests are also areas that you will know a lot about. Perhaps you don't want to mix business and pleasure, but again, investing in an interest area is a good way to manage and mitigate your risk.

You Know Everything You've Learned

We are constantly learning and applying what we have learned to new situations.

What you've learned encompasses both your academic and experiential learning. By focusing your investing activities on ventures with impact that operate in an industry or focus on a subject matter that you have previous knowledge about, you can take one step toward lowering your risk.

Furthermore, imparting your knowledge and sharing it with an entrepreneur and their team is a great way to apply what you have learned and help someone else progress their idea. Knowledge is powerful, and it's what is needed to bring innovations and new business ideas to life.

What have you learned in the school of life, from your travels, and from life's adventures?

Reflect upon what you learned in your formal education. What subjects did you study? What areas of study did you most enjoy or excel at? Consider workshops or short courses that you've taken at some time of your life.

What have you learned from your parents, mentors, teachers, counselors, peers, and friends over the years?

The accumulated learning from your experiences form a vast body of knowledge to which you can refer in order to identify themes and patterns of things that you're really inspired by, motivated about, and driven to do more of.

For example, I studied math and accounting in university and learned about finance in my work. Now I use what I learned to help entrepreneurs improve the financial management of their ventures. Ventures that focus on mathematics education or the financial and investment industries often get my attention because that's an area I have a passion for and knowledge of.

Training as a Ski Instructor: From One Safe Spot to the Next

Years ago, I trained as a downhill ski instructor. I never made a career of it, but I did spend a short time teaching, and I continue to be interested in skiing. In my work in impact investing, I've found many analogies between skiing and investing.

As a ski instructor, I taught people who had never been on skis before how to ski in parallel, and then to carve turns down an intermediate run, by building up their skills and confidence in the steps required. My students learned a set of skills, practicing them repeatedly and in different circumstances until they became acquired skills. Sometimes, standing at the top of a more challenging run, there is a lot of uncertainty and risk. You cannot see the bottom or every obstacle that will appear in your path. But you can see what is in front of you. The approach to navigating and skiing such a run, then, is to go from one safe spot to the next, where you can pause and reevaluate. Your set of acquired skills means that you have tools you can call upon as you move down the mountain.

Investing in private ventures with impact is similar to this approach. You cannot always see what the outcome will be, but equipped with a set of skills, you can move from one safe spot to the next, reevaluating as you go.

Perhaps by day you are a working professional, but on your weekends you spend your time volunteering for an organization that builds affordable homes for low-income families (like Habitat for Humanity). What you've learned on the building site—be it hands-on building and construction knowledge or site management experience—could be the basis for useful advice for a venture tackling affordable housing issues or inclusive construction. Your on-site experience could be invaluable for a young entrepreneur addressing a challenging issue.

Immigrating to Another Country

A subtler example of learning is something I gained through experiential learning. My parents arrived in Canada, where I was born, as immigrants. In

INTEGRATED INVESTING TOOLKIT   111

my adult life, I relocated to another country and became an immigrant to the UK. I found myself frequently entering new communities as the outsider, discovering the lay of the land, and eventually being welcomed into those new communities. This experience, of going from newcomer to welcomed member of a community, taught me something I've applied to new ventures that focus on building communities and welcoming new members from the outside. It is evident in a lot of the work that I do in impact investing, and I'm frequently looking for the exceptions to the rule, the outsiders, and wondering how I can create a culture and community that welcomes them. It is even evident in the impact venture fund I founded. When I found that people who were not extremely wealthy (often described as "not high-net-worth individuals"), many of them women, were excluded from opportunities to invest in private ventures, I created a fund designed to be a way to welcome them into the community of impact venture investors.

The possible examples and situations are vast. The key is to take time and reflect on what you have learned in many different situations, and to look for the themes and patterns in your cumulative learning. You might be surprised by the connections you start to make.

The next step is to take what you've learned and be willing to share it with others—with confidence—to help them progress their ideas. Challenge entrepreneurs and provide them with feedback based on what you have learned and experienced.

Everything you've learned gives you a starting point for identifying areas in which you might be interested in investing.

Who You Know Matters

If you are new to investing in private ventures with impact, knowing other investors and people experienced in identifying and evaluating investment opportunities matters too. It can be helpful to invest with other people.

Investing with experienced investors can expose you to opportunities and help you learn the ropes.

Investor networks are formal, organized groups that identify and often evaluate opportunities together. They are often not-for-profit organizations and, depending upon their size, may have a full-time staff or a volunteer team that hosts network meetings, attracts entre-preneurs to present to the group of investors, and recruits investors to join the network.

Knowing an impact venture fund manager is another approach that can be helpful. If you are a new investor, are limited in the amount of time you can spend on your investing activities, or want to invest in a portfolio of private ventures with impact but do not have enough finan-cial resources to build your own private portfolio, then investing in an impact venture fund may be an option for you.

If you do not know any experienced investors, then look for other people who are interested in learning about impact investing and form an informal group. Investing as part of an informal club is a great way to learn together.

Investing Alongside Experienced Investors

Recall the story about the angel investor from earlier? Not only did he decide to focus on a particular industry in which he had previous work experience, he also sought to invest with others who were more experi-enced in angel investing. He partnered with another investor who had more than twenty years of private equity and venture capital experience, and was also interested in focusing on the health sector. He also sought to invest through angel networks and other groups that were led by investors more experienced than he.

The Integrated Investing Toolkit

In my experience, there are three major questions on investors' minds when they evaluate an investment opportunity:

1. When will I get my money back?
2. What are the potential outcomes from this investment opportunity that will please me?
3. Can I trust the entrepreneur and their team with my money?

The first question is about return *of* capital. The second question is about return *on* capital. Often, the third question is the most important. How the entrepreneur answers the first two questions can provide insight into whether they can be trusted. If the investor can trust the entrepreneur, they will be in a better position to get their money back and get a return on investment. The integrated investing toolkit is designed to help you, the investor, gather the information needed to answer these three major questions.

The toolkit is a combination of traditional investment evaluation tools that are useful and applicable to impact investing; venture development and evaluation tools; and impact identification and evaluation tools.

The traditional investment evaluation tools are a selection of analysis-based approaches that have been used for decades to evaluate investment opportunities. They focus on financial outcomes and commercial impact, so even though they are useful in an impact investing context, they need to be complemented by other tools particular to impact and early-stage venture opportunities. Useful traditional investment evaluation tools include due diligence checklists, scenario analysis, SWOT analysis, and financial analysis.

Venture development and evaluation tools are tools that have been in development since the year 2000. The business model canvas and seven domains model, conceived originally for entrepreneurs starting new ventures to help them design new business models and to evaluate their team, market, and industry as they were just starting out, are just as useful from an investor's perspective.

Impact identification and evaluation tools are new tools that I developed to help impact investors assess the impact of an opportunity. One of the tools is based on the impact concept of access to essential resources that was introduced in Chapter 1. Another tool is a variation of the business model canvas, but with a focus on the impact in each component of a business model. The third impact evaluation tool is a form of cost/benefit analysis that takes into consideration the cost and benefit to a number of different stakeholder groups within and around a venture.

It is the integration of traditional investment evaluation tools, venture development and evaluation tools, and impact identification and evaluation tools that gives you, the integrated investor, a complete set of processes and methods for ascertaining investment opportunities that are a good fit for you and have a good chance of achieving the blended financial and social returns you're looking for. This is the first investment methodology that combines elements from traditional, venture, and impact investment; to date, they have all operated differently. Combining useful tools from each of these investment worlds is a radical new concept that is powerful for you as an integrated investor seeking financial and social returns.

Traditional Evaluation Tools

Traditional investment evaluation tools have been used by people evaluating a wide variety of investment opportunities of all sizes, from opportunities oriented only toward profit to impact investing. Traditional evaluation tools help you gather current and historical information about the entrepreneur, the venture, and the investment opportunity. Some traditional tools, such as analyzing financial projections and scenario analysis, help you evaluate assumptions and to make guesses about what the future might look like for the investment opportunity in front of you.

Traditional evaluation tools rely heavily on analysis and require you to have a benchmark to compare against. Comparing to and contrasting against a benchmark helps you use the information you gather to decide whether the investment opportunity is a good or bad fit for you.

To truly decide if the opportunity is the right fit for you, however, you still need to apply integrated decision making.

DUE DILIGENCE CHECKLISTS

A due diligence checklist is a useful memory aid. It can remind you exactly what information you need to gather from an entrepreneur about them, their team, their venture, and the opportunity they are addressing.

An example due diligence checklist is referenced in the Further Reading section at the end of this book. You may want to add items that you feel would help you in your decision making and tailor a due diligence checklist to meet your specific needs. Bear in mind, though, that it is unlikely you will be able to collect everything on the list. For one, not all the information will be available at such an early stage for a venture. In some cases, not all of it will even be relevant.

Prioritize the information from the due diligence checklist depending upon the opportunity and circumstance to help you answer your major questions.

SCENARIO ANALYSIS

Whereas a due diligence checklist helps you gather current and historical information about an investment opportunity, scenario analysis helps you imagine and evaluate the future of a venture. I think of it as future-oriented research.

While it is impossible to completely predict the future, scenario analysis helps you anticipate possible twists and turns with your venture. It helps you imagine how things might turn out in the short to medium term. The scenarios may or may not happen, but analyzing their potential can help you be prepared.

At the heart of scenario analysis lies the question, "If this happens, then what?" Scenario analysis involves a number of future-oriented questions:

- What if the management team's assumptions come true?
- What if the assumptions you are making about the business come true?
- What if the business exceeds expectations or outperforms the assumptions?
- What if the assumptions do not prove to be true?
- What if you made a different assumption or the management team chose a different route forward?
- What future actions might you have to take to help the business achieve its greatest potential and be successful? What if the management team followed your advice and took those actions?

Scenario analysis is not meant to be exhaustive. It is an opportunity to imagine the future for the business and not take the management team's assumptions, or your own, at face value. Go deeper into the scenario analysis by asking "Then what?" at least three times as you imagine a future path.

ANALYZING FINANCIAL PROJECTIONS

Recall the three main questions on your mind as an investor mentioned earlier in this chapter. Analyzing financial projections prepared by a business's management team can help you answer these questions because projections give an indication of the path the team and the venture are on, including the potential profit, revenues, and other financial measures of progress. With this information, you can make a guess about the current and future valuation of the venture. Financial projections can give you an idea about whether there will be growth in the valuation, and if there is a potential exit. This sheds some light on two of your central questions: When will you get your money back and what outcomes will please me?

For financial projections to be meaningful to you, you need a benchmark or expectation that you can use as a comparison. Potential outcomes that are better than your benchmark or expectation will please you.

When I see that a management team has done their homework and gone through the trouble of preparing intelligent, robust financial projections, I feel that they have thought about the assumptions and factors affecting their business, tested some of them, and are being open about the variables that remain guesses and estimates. This is an early indication of the management team's ability to plan for, manage, and direct the business. It gives me a glimpse into how they make decisions, and gives me greater confidence in the team. It makes me feel I can trust them with my investment.

The assumptions underlying financial projections are just as important as the projections themselves. Look at whether the assumptions are both realistic and ambitious. Are the assumptions and projections exciting? Does the entrepreneur know what has been tested and what is a guess?

Some of the things related to financial projections that you might ask for include the following:

- Past financial performance to date, if it exists
- Two- to three-year projections

Here are questions you can ask about the financial projections:

- What assumptions did the entrepreneur make?
- Have they tested as many assumptions as they could?
- Are they transparent about the unknowns?
- Is there a balance between big vision and realism?
- Do you want to take a leap of faith with the entrepreneur based on the information you have gathered or analyzed?

SWOT ANALYSIS

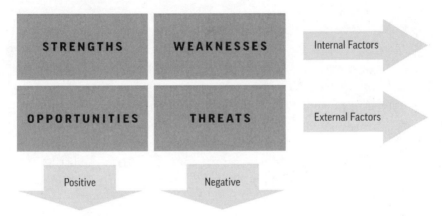

SWOT stands for strengths, weaknesses, opportunities, and threats. It is a risk evaluation tool that helps investors capture the positive and negative aspects of an investment opportunity on a matrix.

Strengths: Think about the positive features of the venture you're evaluating that are internal to the business. Examples could be the experience and track record of the management team, the attractiveness of the venture's product or service, the team's ability to attract customers, the list of customers the business has already attracted, or the impressive group of advisors that surround the venture.

Weaknesses: These are the negative internal features of the venture. Examples of weaknesses to look out for in a venture include gaps in skills and experience within the management team, shortcomings in the product or service, and a lack of basic systems and processes that will allow the business to deliver its products and services.

Opportunities: These are positive factors that are external to the venture—for example, trends amongst significant groups of potential customers. Changes in technology, the economy, society, and political environment that favor the venture's business could also be opportunities.

Threats: External factors with a negative effect on the venture are threats. These include fierce competition, potential downturns in the market the venture is operating in, and economic, societal and political variables that could negatively affect the venture's ability to operate and succeed.

RISK ANALYSIS

Risk analysis entails identifying events or factors that could cause loss of resources, cause delays to desired time frames, jeopardize the success of a project, or circumvent desired outcomes. Risk analysis also includes evaluating the degree of potential risk and identifying ways to mitigate or manage it. Risk analysis is the process of considering the downside of situations and gathering information to make decisions in the event of something undesirable happening.

Below is an example of how information about potential risks can be gathered. When identifying risk, providing some information about its potential impact is helpful for decision making. More importantly, it is best not to leave a risk unaddressed. Thinking ahead about how to mitigate or manage risk, including further information required or next steps to take, helps you be more prepared and enter into an investment relationship with eyes open.

EXAMPLE OF A RISK TABLE

Risk Identified	How to Mitigate or Manage the Risk
Example: highly competitive, crowded industry	Example: patented intellectual property, first mover and leader in the industry, rapid customer adoption
Example: first-time founders, risk of lack of experience	Example: in operation for more than two years, demonstrated ability to attract customers and deliver value and impact

Venture Development and Evaluation Tools

In the 2000s, a methodology and set of tools emerged to help entrepreneurs develop their ventures in a more efficient, lean way. It was called lean startup methodology, and it was created as an attempt to test hypotheses quickly, develop quick prototypes called minimum viable products, and build a startup venture in an agile, responsive, and flexible way, rather than wasting a lot of resources on going down an uncertain path and subsequent failing.

When I encountered this methodology, I thought, *If this is how ventures are now being built, we investors need to make sure our tools for evaluating ventures catch up to the tools the entrepreneurs are using to build them*. I looked at the lean startup methodology and I took two tools I thought would be useful in evaluating ventures as investment opportunities: the business model canvas and the seven domains model.

Getting Started, Starting Lean

In January 2012, I was fortunate to attend a small conference for startup entrepreneurs in London called Leancamp. It convened expert speakers and local entrepreneurs to share knowledge and techniques for developing new ventures using the lean startup methodology and related tools. I was in the early stages of developing Pique Ventures, my impact investment management and consulting business. At that time, I was exploring different investment models and was still in my own customer discovery phase. I hadn't yet decided to build and launch Pique Fund. Not only were the tools I learned at Leancamp useful for me in the development of my own business, they gave me a more in-depth understanding of the venture development challenges and opportunities that entrepreneurs (people that I could be investing in) face, and it gave me insight into tools that would later become useful for the integrated investing toolkit.

The lean startup methodology first started getting attention in 2011 after Eric Ries, an entrepreneur and former chief technology officer for a startup called IMVU, published a book under that name. Lean startup's origins come from the Japanese concept of lean manufacturing, an approach to making products in a customer-focused way. The approach seeks to eliminate any steps from the manufacturing process that are wasteful and do not create value for the end customer. Ries applied and modified the lean approach of manufacturing to starting and growing a business.

At Leancamp, I heard Eric Ries speak, and I also attended talks by Alexander Osterwalder, the co-creator of the business model canvas, and by John Mullins, a professor at the London Business School who developed the seven domains model, author of *The New Business Road Test,* and coauthor of *Getting to Plan B.* I adopted and applied these tools to help investors evaluate businesses as potential investment opportunities.

BUSINESS MODEL CANVAS

The business model canvas[1] was a crowdsourced innovation. To create it, Alexander Osterwalder and Yves Pigneur sought out the perspectives and contributions of 470 business practitioners from forty-five countries. The outcome was a visual representation of nine key components of a company or organization's business model that describes its value proposition, customers, infrastructure, and finances.

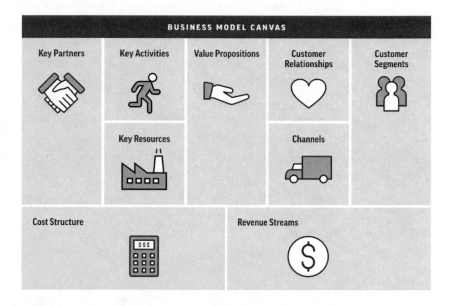

---

1   "Business Model Canvas," Strategyzer AG, accessed April 8, 2016, http://businessmodel generation.com/canvas/bmc. Creative Commons license http://creativecommons.org/licenses/ by-sa/3.0/

The nine key components are described in further detail below:

VALUE:

- Value proposition: The products and services a business offers to meet the needs of its customers. A venture's value proposition is what distinguishes it from its competitors.

CUSTOMERS:

- Customer segment(s): The set or sets of customers that the company is trying to serve. This could be mass market or niche, a specific demographic, or profile of customer. If the venture is trying to serve too many customer segments (or everyone), that's a red flag that it has not figured out who they are actually serving.

- Customer relationships: How the venture interacts with its customers. For example, a customer relationship could be spoken, online, automated, through a community, or co-created.

- Channels: How the venture's products and services reach its customers—that is, the company's distribution channels.

INFRASTRUCTURE:

- Key partners: The other people, businesses, and organizations that the venture needs to deliver its products and services. Key partners can include suppliers, staff and contractors, and other production or delivery partners.

- Key activities: The actions and processes required by the venture and its partners to deliver the products and services. This includes, but is not limited to, production, processing, sales and marketing, and communications.

- Key resources: The materials, inputs, and people power required to deliver the products and services. These resources can be human, financial, physical, and intellectual.

FINANCES:

- Revenue streams: The way a venture generates income from each customer segment—for example, directly selling a product or service, subscription fees, licensing fees, or advertising.

- Cost structure: The expenses and costs of operating the venture, including fixed and variable costs, salaries and wages, and economies of scale or scope.

I like using the business model canvas in my evaluation toolkit because it enables an entrepreneur to quickly communicate their business model to me. For investors, it does require that you have an understanding of different models to compare to (the book *Business Model Generation* provides a number of examples of different types of business models, if you want to learn more). By comparing a venture's business model canvas to other business models you know, you can begin to evaluate whether the business model of the venture you are considering makes sense, whether there are any specific strengths or weaknesses in it, and which components require further investigation.

SEVEN DOMAINS MODEL

The seven domains model was developed by John Mullins, a professor at the London School of Business. It reminds you to look at seven key factors in a venture—factors that Mullins categorizes into three groups: market, industry, and team. There are two market domains (macro and micro), two industry domains (again, macro and micro), and three team domains.

Market Attractiveness: The market is the group of people who are, or will be, buying the product or service delivered by the venture. The market attractiveness domain reminds you to evaluate the size of the market the venture is trying to reach, the total number of potential customers, the value of the sales the venture could generate, and how many products or what volume of services the venture can potentially sell. It's important to evaluate the trends in a given market to determine whether it has grown in recent years, and whether there is a likelihood that it will continue to grow. A more promising investment opportunity is one in which the venture is targeting a growing market rather than a declining one.

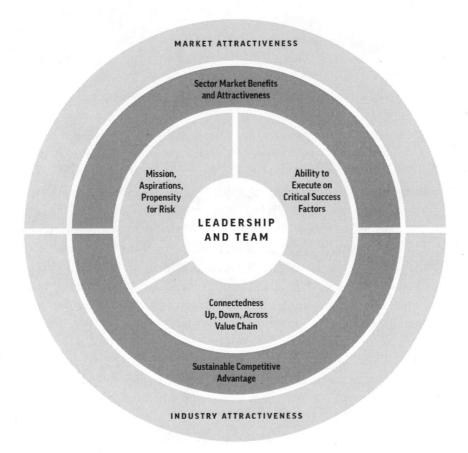

Sector Market Benefits and Attractiveness: Whereas the market attractiveness domain evaluates the market opportunity from a macro perspective, sector market benefits and attractiveness reminds you to evaluate the market opportunity on a micro level. Take a look at the specific (niche) market segment being targeted, and consider how the venture or product differentiates itself from others in the same niche. Consider the other market segments the venture could access. Ask the venture's management team if you can talk to some of their customers as part of your due diligence to gather feedback on their needs and how the venture is meeting them. To gain more insight, consider talking to other customers in the market segment who may be buying from a competitor.

Industry Attractiveness: This domain evaluates the industry on a macro level, considering the barriers to entry the venture is operating within. What is the competitive nature of other participants in the industry? Are competitors numerous and fierce? Are ideas easily stolen? Are there one or a few significant, large competitors who will make it difficult to operate in this industry?

Sustainable Advantage: On a micro level, does the venture have a sustainable advantage that sets it apart? For example, does it have intellectual property that can be or is protected through patents? What are other factors that will make it difficult for others to copy or replicate the venture's products or services?

Mission, Aspirations, and Propensity for Risk: What are the founding team or entrepreneur's mission and aspirations? The strength, audacity, and integrity of an entrepreneur's mission, vision, or goals can be an indicator of the attractiveness of the opportunity. Starting and building a new venture is rife with uncertainty. Therefore, the founding team or entrepreneur must have the appetite and propensity for risk and the desire to navigate risk strategically and intelligently.

Ability to Execute on Critical Success Factors: A key question here is whether the founding team or entrepreneur does what they say they are going to do. Ideas are a dime a dozen, but execution and the ability to actually realize ideas, seize opportunities, and say no to things that do not help the venture succeed is critical.

Connectedness Up, Down, and Across the Value Chain: Does the founding team or entrepreneur have sufficiently strong connections with their customers, suppliers, potential partners, and distribution channels to deliver their value proposition? Connectedness up, down, and across the value chain is a good indicator of the founding team's depth and breadth of experience and network in their chosen field. Are they trusted in the field they are in, or are they fish out of water?

Impact Identification and Evaluation Tools

The final part of the integrated investing toolkit is comprised of tools for identifying and evaluating impact.

ACCESS TO ESSENTIAL RESOURCES MATRIX

In Chapter 1, I introduced the impact concept of access to essential resources. As you start to look at specific companies and ventures and consider whether to invest in them or not, think about all the types of essential resources being provided by the venture. Begin by making a list of them.

Essential Resource	Type of Essential Resource	Who is the Essential Resource for?	Type of Access to the Essential Resource

Let's use the example of myBestHelper, a startup that provides a convenient, technology-enabled service for families to find great caregivers. The company's philosophy is that finding a caregiver is not only a hiring decision, it is like adding an extended family member. It is a major decision to let someone into your home and family life. Caregivers post their profiles on myBestHelper's web-based or mobile-based platform, providing information about their skills and caregiving experience, as well as about their work style, hobbies, and interests, to help give families an idea of whether they would be a good fit. Families who post jobs on the platform, meanwhile, are asked to describe the work and tasks they require, as well as what kind of person they are looking for.

Essential Resource	Type of Essential Resource	Who is the Essential Resource for?	Type of Access to the Essential Resource
Information for finding a caregiver	Decision making	Families, parents	Convenient, efficient, choice
Childcare and caregivers	Managing change, connection	Families, parents	Convenient, efficient, choice
Salaries, wages	Means of exchange	Caregivers, women, newcomers to a country, people new to the workforce	Employment

The access to essential resources matrix, on the next page, is another way to visualize the impact outcomes that could be achieved by the venture you are evaluating.

Types of Access	Basic	Efficient	Choice	Convenient	Supply Chain	Employment
ESSENTIAL RESOURCES FOR Sustenance						
Expression						
Connection						
Managing Change						
Making Decisions						
Exchange						

Here is an example of the matrix completed for the myBestHelper example:

Types of Access	Basic	Efficient	Choice	Convenient	Supply Chain	Employment
ESSENTIAL RESOURCES FOR Sustenance						
Expression						
Connection		X	X	X		
Managing Change		X	X	X		
Making Decisions		X	X	X		
Exchange						X

This shows the many essential resources and types of access that myBestHelper provides, and gives us a starting point for assessing the breadth and depth of the impact. It also tells us what data, metrics, and information we should be gathering to measure this impact.

BUSINESS IMPACT CANVAS

Modeled after the business model canvas, the business impact canvas[1] helps us identify where in a venture's business model there is impact or potential for it.

---

1   Creative Commons license http://creativecommons.org/licenses/by-sa/3.0/

The impact a company has on its stakeholders, customers, suppliers, and broader community can be through the value proposition—that is, the products and services themselves—or the customer segment it is serving (if, for example, it intentionally serves low-income populations or marginalized communities). Its impact can also be in how it reaches and interacts with its customers—for example, by focusing on personal touch.

Impact can also be evident through a company's supply chain by being more sustainable, ethical, or inclusive. Affordability or accessibility are examples of impact through the revenue model or cost structure.

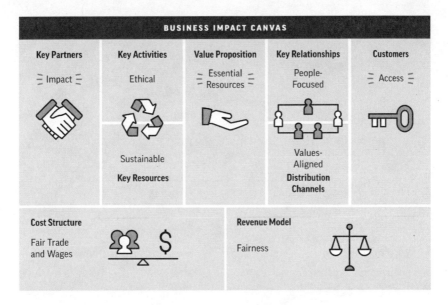

COST/BENEFIT ANALYSIS FOR ALL STAKEHOLDERS

The cost/benefit analysis for all stakeholders is a tool that enables you to examine the cost of a venture to multiple stakeholders, as well as the benefits, in terms of essential resources.

For each type of essential resource provided by the venture you are evaluating, ask yourself, "Does the customer benefit from access to this resource? Do partners, suppliers, employees, the community, and the planet benefit from access to it?" You should also ask yourself whether the venture, its products, services, or activities will represent a cost or any negative impact to stakeholders.

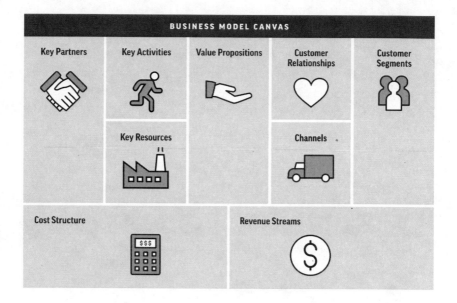

IMPACT SUMMARY

These are the four areas of impact I look for in a venture.

- Business impact
- Social impact
- Qualitative impact
- Macro impact

By categorizing the impact I identify through the tools mentioned above into these four areas, I am able to summarize a venture's impact in a quick, succinct way, paving the way for measuring and assessing the impact with the appropriate systems or tools.

Business impact: These are the more traditional measures of business and commercial success that are easily measured and accounted for, such as profit, sales, and number of customers—typical business metrics.

Social impact: These are measurable shifts and changes directly connected to your business's positive impact. They are quantifiable, discrete changes, such as number of people impacted, number of jobs created, and number of affordable homes developed.

Qualitative impact: Quite often, qualitative impact is what really matters. It is captured intrinsically, emotionally, and intuitively. Such intrinsic-, emotion-, and intuition-based outcomes are practically impossible to measure with numbers, but can be assessed and captured through stories and narrative. Although qualitative impact is often considered intangible, it is nevertheless critical and important.

Macro impact: This captures systems-level change, which is big picture, likely to be indirect, and is therefore harder to measure. Often closely linked with an entrepreneur's vision and mission, macro impact is worthwhile to note and identify, as it can provide direction that influences business in the long term, and social impact in the short term.

Summary

Knowledge, awareness of risk and impact, and the information derived from applying this toolkit give us as much information as is possible at this stage. Now, it's time to get started.

8

INTEGRATED INVESTMENT RELATIONSHIPS

IN 2012, I began building a new business to bring a diverse community of investors together. The business model evolved into Pique Ventures, an impact investment and management company, and Pique Fund, an impact venture fund, which is a private fund that pools investment dollars from several investors.

The way I find investment opportunities has evolved since 2012. Before Pique Fund was formed, when it was still an idea and loosely resembled an investor network, I began looking for entrepreneurs and ventures that could be potential impact investment opportunities. I put out general calls to people in my network by sending e-mails and evaluating almost anyone and anything that was introduced to me as a potential investment opportunity. I spoke at local events and considered entrepreneurs who came to speak with me at those events and the ventures they were building as prospects to be presented to the network of investors I was planning to assemble. I didn't have much of a process, but it was a great way for me to learn. As time went on, I began to develop a smart, effective approach for identifying emerging entrepreneurial leaders and potentially investable ventures.

Soon I started to refine how I would find opportunities. Now my process is different and looks like this:

- I no longer immediately act upon opportunities when I first meet an entrepreneur. Instead, I meet them several times after an initial meeting to see how they've progressed and to begin to test how committed they are to the venture.

- I pass on opportunities that are at the idea stage. Things change quickly, and an idea today may never become an investable venture.

- I get many referrals. I found that entrepreneurs and venture opportunities that were referred to me by people in my network who knew me and whom I trusted, especially other investors, tended to be of better quality; they had been through one stage of vetting already by the person who referred them.

- I began to track and follow entrepreneurs and ventures that I was interested in. Rather than wait for entrepreneurs to come to me, I started to keep my eye on people who I thought were interesting and had the potential to be strong leaders in their field.

This approach to finding opportunities is centered on the intention to form investment relationships over time. As with anything, honing your integrated investing skills requires practice. In this chapter, I'll walk you through some places to start investing and how to start building investment relationships, as well as some of the common forms of documenting investment relationships.

Getting Started

The world of investors is typically split into accredited investors and retail investors. The types of investments available differ for each type.

To be an accredited investor doesn't mean you need to pass an exam or be certified by a third-party organization. Instead, it means you must satisfy criteria set by an investment regulatory body. In the US, this is the Securities and Exchange Commission; in Canada, it is a provincial securities commission.[1] Accredited investor criteria typically apply to corporations, trusts, banks, and individuals, and are usually based on a minimum net worth or annual income threshold.

In the US, an accredited investor is defined in the Securities Act of 1933 as someone who has individual net worth (or joint net worth with their spouse) that exceeds $1 million at the time of investing in the securities of a company. A person's net worth, for the purposes of the accredited investor definition, excludes the value of their primary residence. Alternatively, there is an income-based definition of accredited investor, which is an individual with income exceeding $200,000 in each of the two most recent years, or a joint income with a spouse exceeding $300,000 for those years, and a reasonable expectation of the same income level in the current year. So in the US, you can be an accredited investor based on minimum net worth or minimum annual income. Accredited investor definitions may differ from country to country, but most typically have similar criteria.

Retail investors, on the other hand, are individuals who meet neither the net worth threshold nor the income threshold. Retail investors are sometimes referred to as non-accredited investors, and are not permitted to invest in private investment offerings. In some countries, and certain provinces of Canada, retail investors can invest in the private offerings of their friends and family—but this isn't legal in the US.[2] Retail investors can access private impact investing opportunities only if the investment products have been designed for retail investors and meet certain regulatory requirements.

The average person is a retail investor and not an accredited investor. Because of this, it is difficult for them to access impact investment opportunities, particularly in private companies. The regulations were originally designed to protect investors from fraud and scams, but in my opinion, they now create an inequality in access to investment oppor-

---

1   In the UK, the relevant statutory instrument is the Financial Services and Markets Act 2000 (Financial Promotion) Order 2005, accessed April 8, 2016, http://www.legislation.gov.uk/uksi/2005/1529/pdfs/uksi_20051529_en.pdf.

2   In some cases, non-accredited investors who are sophisticated, experienced, and knowledgeable enough to evaluate the risks and rewards of a private investment opportunity are permitted to invest. Do consult a lawyer to understand the details of the securities law and applicable exemptions.

tunities. Whereas accredited investors have access to a wide variety of investment types, retail investors are limited. Fortunately, the investment landscape is changing—but it's happening slowly. I talk more about this in the section below on investing through a crowdfunding portal.

One of the best ways to start investing is with others. Alternatively, you can invest directly in ventures on your own by identifying and contacting entrepreneurs directly, evaluating opportunities, and conducting due diligence. There are many benefits to investing with a group. It gives you the chance to meet other investors, learn from their experiences, and possibly be mentored by them, and you get to share the effort and work. Research by Rob Wiltbank for the Kauffman Foundation in 2007 showed that investment returns were higher when at least twenty hours of due diligence and evaluation on a private venture were performed; the more hours spent, the better the returns.[1] A group of investors can share and split the work that goes into due diligence, saving you time, money, and effort.

Investment Clubs

An investment club is an informal way for investors to organize themselves in a group and invest together. Clubs focused on investing in private ventures are presently limited to accredited investors. Retail investors can organize themselves into an investment club and invest in publicly traded stocks and bonds of values-based companies or invest in mutual fund units. Members of an investment club might identify investment opportunities together, or work off the strengths and expertise of individual members. If one or more members of the investment club have more experience identifying opportunities or has greater access to deal flow through their network, it may be advantageous to rely more heavily on that member's connections.

The main benefit of an investment club is the flexibility in the amount you invest and the goals of the club. The key is finding or forming the

---

1   Robert Wiltbank, PhD and Warren Boeker, PhD, "Returns to Angel Investors in Groups" (Ewing Marion Kauffman Foundation, 2007), accessed April 8, 2016, http://sites.kauffman.org/pdf/angel_groups_111207.pdf. The 538 angels included in a study by the Kauffman Foundation enjoyed 2.6X returns over the life of their investments. For deals on which collective due diligence totaled less than twenty hours, returns were only 1.1X. But deals on which angels put in over forty hours of due diligence (the top quartile) returned 7.1X to those investors.

right group for you. The challenges of an investment club are in finding the right fit and mix of people that you feel comfortable and aligned with. You need to find people you trust and get along with, and make sure that there is a mix of people with diverse backgrounds to cover different aspects of running the club and evaluating investment opportunities. Ideally you want a group of people who can also learn from each other.

The National Association of Investors Corporation[1] provides resources to people in the US who want to join or form an investment club.

The following are the key features of an investment club, and the steps to forming one:

- Gather a minimum number of people together to invest as a group, create a big enough pool of investment dollars, and have enough variety of experience and connections for deal flow.

- Set a schedule for meeting regularly.

- Take the time to get to know each other as investors, especially if you aren't well acquainted. Clubs might form with people who already know each other and are friends, or with one central person who is the mutual connection for all the members. It may start with a couple of people getting together and bringing some other friends along with them. In all cases, though, knowing someone in a business or social capacity is different from investing with them, so it is worth spending the time to get to know each other as investors.

- Encourage everyone in the club to share with the group what their individual and mutual goals are.

- Have a candid conversation early in the formation of the club about how much each person is willing to invest.

- Designate someone as the club manager and identify another person as their backup.

- Keep good records and have a system of keeping track of when members joined the club and how much they will invest. Keep track of what the club invests in.

---

1   "BetterInvesting Investment Clubs," BetterInvesting, accessed April 8, 2016, http://www.betterinvesting.org/Public/Clubs/default.htm.

- Set out investment criteria.

- Establish and then follow processes to identify opportunities, for due diligence, and for decision making.

- Set deadlines and clear goals for investing—for example, make five investments in as many months.

Angel Investor Networks

A more formal approach to organizing investors as a group is the angel investor network. At present, they are typically only available for accredited investors to join.

An angel investor network is an organization that accredited investors can join as members. Employed or volunteer network managers convene meetings where entrepreneurs are invited to present their ventures and the opportunity of investing to network members.

They often require an annual membership fee and may require their members to make a minimum investment into a venture that is presented to the group. The minimum investment can be as low as $10,000, but read the fine print carefully—there may be a requirement to invest that amount annually.

Investors' Circle is the largest, oldest investor network in North America that's focused on impact investing. In 2010, a new national network of impact investors, Toniic, was formed.

Investing via a Crowdfunding Portal

In 2012, the Jumpstart Our Business Startups Act (or JOBS Act, for short) was passed in the United States with a primary goal of fostering entrepreneurship, job creation, and economic growth. The passing of the JOBS Act also signified a first step toward making investing in private ventures more accessible to the average American citizen. There is still a long road ahead toward change in the way investment opportunities in private companies are accessed, but the JOBS Act is a start.

At the time of writing, the new rules for investing in private companies are still evolving. Title III of the JOBS Act created rules under securities law that enables companies to sell shares and other securities through crowdfunding, which is described by the US Securities and Exchange Commission (SEC) as a financing method in which money is raised through soliciting relatively small individual investments or contributions from a large number of people. The new rules enable a more diverse group of people to invest in private investment offerings; however, the SEC places limits on how much someone can invest in a twelve-month period based on their income and net worth.[1]

Retail investors in all Canadian provinces except for Ontario can already invest in private companies, if the company issues an offering memorandum, a document that details the risks, rewards, and other pertinent information of the investment offering. This document helps prospective investors make an informed decision about whether they should invest. Startup crowdfunding securities legislation was also passed in Canada in 2015. Such opportunities can be accessed directly through contact with the company seeking investment or through intermediaries known as exempt market dealers.

In response to the changes to the regulations and legislation in the US and in an effort to make investing in private ventures more accessible in Canada, online equity crowdfunding platforms have emerged.

To be clear, these online equity crowdfunding platforms are not to be confused with donation and reward-based models such as Kickstarter, Indiegogo, Kiva, and other similar platforms. Kickstarter and Indiegogo are two online platforms where people who pledge financial support for creative projects receive perks or products in exchange for their monetary gifts. Kiva is a not-for-profit microfinance portal that enables people to provide loans to entrepreneurs—in some cases in very small amounts—but does not provide these lenders with a financial return on their loan. Kiva is essentially a donation-based model, but there is a chance that the principal of the microfinance loan will be recycled and lent to other entrepreneurs or repaid to the lender.

Equity crowdfunding portals endeavor to be platforms where people can support private business ventures by providing financial support in exchange for shares or other equity-type securities in the private business ventures. They present an opportunity for investors to access deal flow and identify investment opportunities. Regulatory bodies are currently carefully reviewing and establishing the rules on how equity

---

1   For the most up-to-date information on securities laws and regulations, visit the US Securities and Exchange Commission website at www.sec.gov.

crowdfunding portals operate in an effort to protect investors from potentially fraudulent activities.

The equity crowdfunding space is evolving and ever-changing. Emerging platforms to keep an eye on include AngelList, Crowdfunder, and CircleUp. Even reward-based stalwart Indiegogo has announced that it is exploring throwing its hat into the equity crowdfunding ring in the future.

Investing in a Fund

People with more financial resources can invest through a fund. A fund is a legal entity in which investment dollars from a number of investors can be pooled. In the context of integrated investing, I'm talking about a fund where the money is invested in private ventures. Such a fund could be referred to as an impact investment fund if it is focused specifically on impact-based ventures, a seed fund if it is focused specifically on ventures at an early stage of development (money invested at the early stage of development of a business is often referred to as seed capital, hence the name "seed fund"), or a venture fund.

A private investment fund is not a mutual fund. It is not regulated or sold to investors in the same way. It is still a private investment, but like a mutual fund, a seed fund is managed by a fund manager.[1] The fund manager does more of the on-the-ground work so that you don't have to.

Even though a fund manager will be doing more of the daily investment identification and evaluation, the integrated investing techniques will still be useful for you in evaluating both a fund and the people who manage it. Instead of identifying many opportunities to invest in and evaluating at least twenty opportunities to ensure you build a diversified portfolio, when investing in a fund you're likely to identify a much smaller number of funds to invest in, maybe even only one, and the diversification comes from how the fund manager builds the portfolio. This

---

1   A fund is a legal entity for the purposes of pooling or aggregating capital from investors. Typical legal entity structures for funds are a corporation limited by shares or a limited partnership. There is always a fund manager managing the capital in the fund and the business affairs of the fund. It could be an individual or a team of people or a fund management company. Contrast this with angel investors, who are individuals investing their own money directly into companies and managing their own capital.

approach to investing requires that you apply the evaluation tools from the integrated investing toolkit to assess the fund and the fund manager and determine whether you trust them with your investment dollars.

Working with Your Financial Advisor

If you're a retail investor, you can still put the integrated investing techniques to work and begin to practice a more integrated approach to working with your financial advisor and investing in mutual funds and publicly traded stocks and bonds.

The foundational pieces of integrated investing, such as the impact concept of access to essential resources, reflecting on why you invest in the first place, how your values play a role in investing, and how to make integrated investment decisions, are just as applicable to choosing the right financial advisor to work with or evaluating and selecting the right mutual funds, stocks, or bonds to invest in.

Resources and Investment Opportunities

Investment opportunities are subject to change. The ones mentioned below were active at the time of writing and illustrate the types of opportunities that may be available.

An example of a regionally specific opportunity is SolarShare, a renewal energy cooperative based in Canada. SolarShare[1] periodically offers an impact investment bond directly to investors and is available only to residents of Ontario.

ImpactSpace[2] is an online aggregator of information about companies, investors, deals, and people in the global impact investing industry.

AngelList connects startups, investors, and people looking for employment opportunities at startups. Accredited investors can invest in startups through the online platform and can also lead investment syndicates, enabling other people to co-invest with them. Investors are able to filter for social ventures and impact investing opportunities.[3]

---

1   "Invest," SolarShare, accessed April 9, 2016, http://www.solarbonds.ca/invest/invest.

2   "About Us," ImpactSpace, accessed April 9, 2016, http://impactspace.com/about.

3   "Ventures for Good Startups," AngelList, accessed April 9, 2016, https://angel.co/ventures-for-good.

In response to the emergence and the increasing demand for equity crowdfunding, svx and FrontFundr are two platforms in Canada that are presently growing. svx, which specifically has an impact investing focus, is an online platform that helps connect accredited investors with impact ventures and funds in the province of Ontario. FrontFundr describes itself as a bridge to connect investors and entrepreneurs. FrontFundr provides new and experienced investors access to screened investment pitches and helps early-stage companies access the new capital market.

The present challenge to making resources about impact investing opportunities available to investors is ensuring that information about investment offerings is up-to-date. Scaling and growing platforms and regulatory issues are also obstacles. For example, the Centre for Social Innovation in Toronto, a co-working space, community, and launch pad for change makers and innovators, recently offered a community bond to investors, but when this book went to print, it was closed to new investors. MicroPlace, a regulated, online broker/dealer for microfinance opportunities owned by eBay, had trouble scaling its business and decided to stop offering new sales of investments as of January 2014.

If you are interested in reading more information about the current status of equity crowdfunding investment opportunities for retail investors, two resources include the following:

- National Crowdfunding Association of Canada,[1] a not-for-profit association focused on supporting, educating, researching, leading, and developing the social and Investment crowdfunding industry in Canada

- Crowdsourcing.org, a website that gathers and provides news, articles, videos, and site information on the topic of crowdsourcing and crowdfunding. On topics specifically related to equity crowdfunding, search for the key words "equity crowdfunding"

---

1   "About Us," National Crowdfunding Association of Canada, accessed April 9, 2016, http://ncfacanada.org/about-us/.

Building an Investment Relationship

I recall a situation where a colleague, Sharon, was beginning to take greater interest in her personal investment portfolio and the decisions she was making. After speaking with me, she developed an interest in investing in private ventures and started to pay more attention to and seek out entrepreneurs starting new businesses. She met a young entrepreneur, a recent university graduate, who was developing a venture that she liked the sound of. She asked me what I thought about it. I had not met the entrepreneur. I told my colleague that the first thing I would ask myself was whether this person was a leader. Could they lead and run a business? Did they have that potential? The next thing I would ask was why them, and why this business? I wondered what connections, business relationships, and experience they had that could enable them to be successful in starting and growing the venture. These were the kinds of questions she needed to be able to answer as part of evaluating an entrepreneur and the beginnings of building an investment relationship.

The success of a private venture depends highly upon the entrepreneur and the team leading the venture. Successful investing in private ventures depends highly upon evaluating the entrepreneur and building the investment relationship. Every new venture faces a lot of uncertainty, growth, and change; as an investor, you want someone at the helm whom you can trust, who can make good decisions in the face of uncertainty, and who will be communicative with their investors through good times and bad times.

Investing is a people-focused activity, and it is helpful to have a relationship mindset (as opposed to a transaction mindset). Building an investment relationship takes time and effort, but the following tips will help you find a productive path, one where you'll get to learn more about the entrepreneur and your own investing style along the way.

Networking and Referrals

To get the most exposure to investment opportunities in this space, start by spending time with people who are actively working in, talking about, and investing in the impact venture sector. Speak with friends who are business owners or building entrepreneurial ventures.

On Meetup.com, look for events in your local area by searching for the key words "impact investing." Key words such as "social enterprise," "social venture," and "startup investing" might also bring up some interesting groups, but these are likely to be more focused on entrepreneurs than investors.

Conferences centered on impact investing and social ventures usually attract accredited investors, entrepreneurs, consultants, business advisors, and anyone interested in the field. Some conferences, such as SOCAP, Social Venture Network, Net Impact, TBLI Conference, Social Finance Forum (Canada), and Good Deals (UK), draw large audiences, and it can be daunting to attend one for the first time, especially if you don't know anyone there. I highly recommend attending a smaller, local event first, and then making plans to attend the larger conferences with someone you know or with specific goals of hearing a particular speaker or panel.

Local organizations or local chapters of national organizations frequently host events to build their local impact investing community, convene people, and share information and knowledge about the field:

- Ashoka (http://usa.ashoka.org/ashoka-and-cities)
- Acumen (http://plusacumen.org/chapters)
- Impact Hub (http://www.impacthub.net/where-are-impact-hubs)
- Slow Money (https://slowmoney.org and https://slowmoney.org/local-groups/)

Meeting Entrepreneurs, Discovering Ventures

Investing in a venture can give you the opportunity to get closer to meeting the people who are actually leading and building tomorrow's businesses, in particular if you invest as a member of an investment club or an angel investor network. You won't always get to meet the entrepreneur in person, especially if you are investing via a crowdfunding portal, a fund, or a financial advisor. But it is advantageous for you to meet entrepreneurs to get more exposure to the variety of business founders and ventures out there.

If you're new to entrepreneurship and ventures, meeting these people will help familiarize you with their language, their needs, and the opportunities and challenges they face while building a business. Ask them questions about their experience as business leaders, about their business itself, and about any changes they are going through. Find out how they are taking advantage of the opportunities in front of them and how they are dealing with challenges in or around their business.

If you are an entrepreneur yourself, this experience of meeting other entrepreneurs with an investor's perspective is a great way to get accustomed to evaluating others and looking at business from a new perspective. Investing in a business is different from building one from the inside as a founder. As an investor, you are not the CEO of the business you're investing in, someone else is, so you need to practice and gain experience in evaluating the potential of others to lead and manage their new business well.

Develop a relationship with the entrepreneurs you're considering investing in. Imagine what it would be like going through good times and bad with them.

Meeting an Entrepreneur: Integrated Investment Decision Making Starts Here

It is never too early to put integrated decision making to work. After an initial meeting with an entrepreneur, you have the opportunity to practice these new tools. What information from analysis, emotion, body, and intuition were you able to gather from your initial meeting? How will that information guide you? Do they tell you that you should meet the entrepreneur again? What do they tell you about the venture?

Experiential Due Diligence

The integrated investing toolkit discussed in Chapter 7 was comprised of a number of evaluation tools, including due diligence techniques. When evaluating an entrepreneur or the management team of a venture and building a relationship with them, you want to undertake something that I call experiential due diligence. This is a method of evaluating a person's abilities, skills, and character through actual exposure, contact, and interaction.

I always put experiential due diligence into practice when I meet and speak with entrepreneurs. I start to get a sense of how they make decisions, how they approach opportunities, and how they deal with setbacks. When providing constructive feedback or criticism, experiential due diligence enables me to assess how the entrepreneur deals with conflict.

After spending time with an entrepreneur and experiencing how they do things over a period of time, I'm able to get a stronger sense of their motivations and direction. Are they just in it for themselves, or do they want to build a mutually beneficial investment relationship with me or investors in general? Experiential due diligence is to investment relationships as dating and courting someone is to romantic relationships. You need to get to know each other before entering into a long-term, committed partnership.

Here are my top tips for building an investment relationship:

- Build relationships with entrepreneurs over time.

- Keep in mind the mindsets of integrated investing (abundance, curiosity, exchange, relationship, future potential, and resources). For example, seek out mutual relationships founded with a mindset of exchange: you help them, they help you.

- Get a sense of whether there is a mutual desire to work together. For me, a conversation with an entrepreneur that gives me a feeling of positive energy and a strong sense that we are on the same path is an early signal that there is the potential for building an investment relationship. This sense is often unspoken, but we can tell we really like each other and have mutual respect for each other's projects.

- Ask tough questions and be confident about challenging any assumptions the entrepreneurs might be making. How an entrepreneur responds to challenges is very informative. You want to know how the entrepreneur handles tougher times.

- Be clear about what you're asking for in the investment relationship. If you are seeking a specific outcome, let the entrepreneur know. If you have a timing constraint, speak up and share that information.

Hearing the Pitch

As an investor, I frequently hear pitches from entrepreneurs. Sometimes they are delivered in an informal way, such as in conversation at an event or in a coffee meeting. On other occasions, the pitches are more formal—for example, presentations made to a group of investors at an angel network meeting.

Initial meetings, often where you first hear the pitch, are not for deciding whether to invest money in the entrepreneur and their venture, but rather to determine whether you want to meet them again, whether there is potential fit and values alignment, and whether you should invest time in building a relationship with them. The pitch is likely to be brief—in fact, it may take less than ten minutes. The information provided by the entrepreneur may be limited. The intention of the pitch is to give you a first impression and some preliminary information about the entrepreneur and their venture. After hearing them speak, your job is to decide whether to meet them again and gather more information. It's generally a good idea to keep initial meetings brief—twenty to thirty minutes—so that you don't invest too much time too early.

What you can expect when you first hear an entrepreneur's pitch can vary, but to give you an idea, here is a summary of what they might tell you:

- A bit about themselves (and their cofounders, if they're a part of a team)

- Something about their product or service (don't get too hung up on whether you would be their customer; instead, look for them to show you that there are customers for their product or service—that there is demand, or that they are well on their way to validating customer demand)

- Some general information about their business—who else is on their team and what their plans are for growing; a summary of their operations, business infrastructure, and systems in anticipation of the next stages of development and growth; and how they plan to grow their business

- What they are trying to achieve, and what they need to do so

The information presented in a pitch is introductory and highly summarized. You should focus on whether you are intrigued and interested enough to want to find out more about the opportunity and continue the conversation. It's like peeling an onion. Spend a small amount of time finding out some key information to decide whether to peel back a layer and delve deeper.

Take the opportunity to ask the entrepreneur questions after their pitch—or during, if the pitch is more conversational. Here are some of the questions you could ask:

- Why did you decide to start the business?

- What is your vision and mission?

- Are you getting any help from advisors or mentors in developing your business? Were you part of an incubator or accelerator program?

- Who is using your product or service, and how many people are using it?

- Do you have any paying customers? How many, and what is the feedback from them?

- What are your next steps in developing and growing your business? What kind of support do you need?

Each time you meet, find out more information, and ask the entrepreneur to update you and demonstrate the progress they have made. Find out what they have achieved in the time that has passed since you last met, what new information they have gathered in the process of building their venture, and what challenges they presently face.

At some point after hearing the pitch, building the relationship, and seeing some progress made, decide whether the investment opportunity is compelling enough to do formal and detailed due diligence (using the integrated investing toolkit). Get references from other people who have invested in the entrepreneurs previously or in their current venture, or who have worked with them previously. Speak with their customers and with people in their supply chain.

Power Poses and Power Pitches

Does the entrepreneur present herself confidently? Is she sitting back and looking disinterested? Are you leaning forward into the conversation in interest or do you have your arms folded? Our body language says a lot about the confidence we have in what we're talking about and how we present ourselves. The body language of the entrepreneur who's pitching you can be an indicator of how confident they are in their venture and abilities. Your own body language can signal whether you are interested in or attracted to the opportunity they're presenting to you.

Recall from Chapter 5 the research by Amy Cuddy, a professor and researcher at Harvard Business School. She studies how non-verbal behavior and snap judgments affect people from the classroom to the boardroom. In her TED Talk, "Your Body Language Shapes Who You Are," she describes how power poses can affect your stress levels, perception of risk, and mindset. Body language affects our communication and decision making, both of which are critical activities for the entrepreneurs making the pitch and for the investors hearing it. For more insights on body language, communication, and power poses, take a look at her TED Talk.

One-Pagers and Investor Decks

Before you meet an entrepreneur, or maybe as a takeaway after your first meeting with them, you may receive an executive summary about the venture and the investment opportunity. It could be as brief as one page (hence referred to as a "one pager"), or it could be several pages. When the entrepreneur presents their pitch to you, it may be delivered unaccompanied by any materials, or you might see a set of presentation slides—an "investor deck," or simply a "deck"—from an entrepreneur (usually in a more formal pitch).

A twelve-slide deck might contain some combination of the following information:

1. Name and elevator pitch (value proposition)
2. Problem

3. Solution (value proposition)
4. Market validation (evidence of potential demand)
5. Market size
6. Product (value proposition)
7. Business model (revenue model)
8. Market adoption (customer channels)
9. Competition
10. Competitive advantages
11. Team
12. Investment requirement

If, after meeting an entrepreneur and hearing their pitch, you believe you could work with them and potentially invest in them and their venture, the next step in the investment relationship is to perform thorough due diligence and evaluation. At this stage, you will put the integrated investing toolkit to use to evaluate the entrepreneur, the venture, and the investment opportunity in detail. This includes, but is not limited to, the business model, the team's capabilities, the competitive environment, the business's impact, the risk involved, and the financial projections associated with the venture.

Common Forms of Investment

Up to this point, we have been talking about evaluating the entrepreneur and building the investment relationship. We'll now move on to a high-level summary of the legal side of things. Legal agreements represent and document the terms and conditions of the relationship, which are legally binding and enforceable. In the investment relationship, they are like a pre-nuptial and marriage contract. Before entering into the investment, get legal and tax advice! Talk to your lawyer about the details of the legal agreements that are required for the specific situation and the investment opportunities you'll be looking at.

To give you a bit of background on the forms that an investment in a private venture could take, I'm going to cover some of the common structures that are used for investing in equity.

Common Shares

Common shares align you with the entrepreneurs who founded and started the business. Other people who were involved early on in the inception and building of the business may also have common shares. Common shares are the most risky form of investment since there is no pre-specified time when you'll get your original invested capital back or an investment return. Your investment return is dependent upon the future acquisition of your shares—by a larger company, by the general public through an initial public offering, by other investors, or by the management team or employees of the business. The potential for your shares to be acquired in the future is dependent upon the attractiveness of the business, including the growth in its revenues and profitability, and the impact it has on people.

Convertible Debt

Convertible debt is a type of loan or promissory note with an option to convert into equity shares later after a trigger event. Conversion to equity means the amount of money you invest is converted, at a certain share price referred to as a conversion price, into a purchase of shares of the company.

Valuation and Determining a Share Price

Valuation of private companies is an extensive topic. It makes up a profession of its own and is the subject of many other books. I won't go into detail about how to value a private company in this book. However, it would be good idea for you to have some understanding of valuation and how it impacts share prices and conversion prices for an investment in a private company.

Arbitrary Share Price

Take, for example, a company with one million shares issued and outstanding and the management and board of the company set an arbitrary share price of $0.25 per share. A million shares at $0.25 per share means an implied valuation of $250,000.

Percentage Ownership and Valuation

More often that not, investment in a private company is referred to by the percentage of equity of the company you own and its valuation. For example, say a company is willing to exchange 10% of its ownership for $250,000 of investment. The implied valuation is determined by dividing $250,000 by 10% to arrive at a valuation of $2.5 million. Over time, as the company raises more investment, your percentage ownership might decrease, which is referred to as dilution. The expectation is that the company is raising more investment and continuing to grow, such that the valuation goes up. As an investor, you want the valuation to go up! Let's say your ownership has been diluted to 2.5% by other investments into the company after five years, but the valuation of the company has increased to $25 million. Your share of the company would now be valued at $625,000 (2.5% × $25 million). Bear in mind that these are just examples to illustrate what might happen to your percentage ownership and the company's valuation. Actual outcomes from your investment will be different.

Convertible Debt and Conversion Price

In the case of a convertible debt investment, the amount you invested may be converted to equity at a future date. The share price and valuation concepts mentioned above might be applied, but there are some other features to the convertible debt. The convertible debt may specify a cap on valuation. This is the maximum valuation that your investment will convert at. The convertible debt may also specify a discount on valuation. For example, if you invested $100,000, are entitled to a 25% future discount, and the company is valued at $1 million in a future financing, your investment would instead convert based on a valuation of $750,000. So instead of getting 10% ownership, you would get 13.3%.

The typical features of convertible debt include the following:

- Term of one to two years

- Accrues interest at a specified percentage (and is included in the amount that is converted to equity shares later on; the interest is typically not paid out in cash, unless you negotiate otherwise)

- Option to convert the amount you invested from a loan to equity shares automatically at the end of the loan term or when a subsequent round of financing is raised by the company

- If no valuation or valuation cap is specified in the terms of the convertible debt, option to delay the negotiation about the valuation and price of equity shares until a subsequent round of financing

- At the end of the term, if the company hasn't raised a subsequent round of financing, depending upon the terms of the convertible note, you, the investor, could seek to be repaid in full, keep the loan outstanding, or convert to equity

- All of these terms can be negotiated differently depending upon what you, the entrepreneur, and other investors want and agree to.

Preferred Shares

Preferred shares are a type of equity share that gives an investor a percentage ownership in a private company. Unlike holders of common shares, the holders of these shares get preferential rights, which may include the following:

- Deciding who is on the board of directors of the company

- Voting rights, meaning they have greater influence over decisions made at the shareholder level of the company

- Dividend preference, meaning dividends owed to them get paid out before those to common shareholders

- Liquidation preference, meaning that in the event the company is sold, they will get paid back before common shareholders

- Other rights including, but not limited to, influencing how the company is managed, how management and staff are paid, and how shares can be sold or transferred

Other New Forms of Investment

Simple Agreement for Future Equity

In December 2013, Y Combinator, a company that provides seed funding for startups and helps accelerate their development by focusing on helping the founders make desirable products, launched a new form of financing they referred to as a "simple agreement for future equity," or SAFE for short. While it is increasingly being adopted by investors in Silicon Valley, it is still not widely used across the US, Canada, and in other locations. I mention it here in case you come across it. Common shares, convertible debt, and preferred shares are still the most typical and common forms of investment that you'll encounter.

SAFE is a form of convertible equity and has the following features:

- A SAFE is a form of equity financing and is not debt; like shares, a SAFE does not have a maturity date.

- A SAFE does not accrue interest. The investment returns on a SAFE are dependent upon the future success and valuation of the company.

Revenue-Based Financing

Revenue-based financing is a financing structure where a company promises to pay a percentage of its future revenues to an investor in exchange for capital investment. The total amount that is paid back to an investor is based on a multiple of the initial capital investment. A number of early-stage venture funds and accelerators—including Seattle-based Lighter Capital and Fledge, and Vancouver, Canada-based TIMIA Capital—offer revenue-based financing. It is an increasingly attractive structure for impact-based businesses as there is less need for company founders to exit their venture through an acquisition in order to provide their investors with a return. Revenue-based financing enables founders to stay with their business long-term whilst providing investment returns through a structured, methodical buy back of shares or payback of capital over time.

Investing with other people gives you access to their experience and access to more information about investment opportunities. But it is not just information about the ventures you want; you also want to gather information about the entrepreneurs you might be investing in. A key part to building an investment relationship is putting in the time to get to know an entrepreneur. Once you find some entrepreneurs and investment opportunities that you are interested in pursuing, applying the techniques from the integrated investing toolkit and from integrated decision making will help you decide whether to go move forward. Understand the different forms of investments that are possible, and seek advice from your lawyer and financial advisor about any legal agreements and investment terms you're considering entering into before signing on the dotted line.

Honing your integrated investing skills requires practice. I encourage you to continue to refer to the resources in this book as you start to meet other investors and entrepreneurs building meaningful, purposeful businesses of the future.

9

GENDER LENS INVESTING

J OSS WHEDON, AN American screenwriter, director, and producer, best known as the creator of the television series *Buffy the Vampire Slayer* and *Firefly*, puts it best. When asked yet again why he writes strong women characters, he answered poignantly: because people still ask him that question.

Rarely a day goes by that I don't read about gender inequity or imbalance in the workplace, on boards, in the C-Suite and leadership positions in general, in STEM (science, technology, engineering, and math), amongst venture capitalists and angel investors, and in the media.

We have organizations like Catalyst, which works with businesses and the professions to build inclusive environments and expand opportunities for women at work; the Representation Project, a not-for-profit organization that produced the film *Miss Representation*, documenting the negative portrayal of women in media; and the Everyday Sexism Project, which catalogues and shares through social media instances of sexism experienced by women on a day-to-day basis. But these barely scratch the surface of injustices constantly being perpetrated against women on a global scale.

Some prominent news and media outlets have sections dedicated to women. The British national daily newspaper *The Guardian* has the Women's Blog,[1] online news and blog post aggregator Huffington Post has a Women section,[2] and global speaking conference TED hosts an annual event, TEDWomen, specifically about the power of women and girls to be creators and change makers (incidentally, the two largest newspapers in the US, the *Wall Street Journal* and *The New York Times*, do not have dedicated sections focused on women's issues, though the *Wall Street Journal* does have a Task Force for Women in the Economy). Canada has a federal government organization called Status of Women Canada that promotes equality for women and their full participation in the economic, social, and democratic life of Canada.

In this chapter, I share with you my own experience of gender equity and inequity, explain what gender lens investing is, why it is important, and how you can use it. It is written from the perspective of being a woman in the context of investing and does not get into broader, more complex issues of gender.

My Experience of Gender Equity and Inequity

I remember huddling around a then-shiny new computer called PET in a small room in the basement of my elementary school in the early 1980s. I was eight or nine, and was learning how to code in an old programming language called BASIC. At the time, there was no such thing as a girls-only code camp. We had this opportunity to learn how to code because we were schoolchildren, and the technology and equipment were relatively new.

I had an early experience of gender differences during Art Summer Camp in Toronto when I was twelve. Our group was taken on a field trip to the Art Gallery of Ontario, where a friend and I noticed the disproportionate number of paintings of nude women versus paintings of nude

---

1 "The women's blog," *The Guardian*, accessed April 9, 2016, http://www.theguardian.com/lifeandstyle/womens-blog.

2 "Huffpost Women," *Huffington Post*, accessed April 9, 2016, http://www.huffingtonpost.com/women.

men. We asked our camp leader why this was the case. His reasoning was that the nude female form was considered more beautiful. It wasn't an answer that my friend and I found satisfactory, but we left it at that.

I attended high school between 1987 and 1992, and during that period I was oblivious to gender inequity. My primary focus was to learn as much as I could about the subject areas I was most interested in, and I believed that hard work and good grades, not my gender, were what mattered. I felt that the learning environment at my school was supportive; I don't recall being treated any differently because I was a woman. My attitude and beliefs about gender equity continued in the five years after high school I spent at university.

I graduated from university in 1997, armed with bachelor of mathematics and master of accounting degrees, and subsequently pursued my first career as a Chartered Accountant (a professional designation in Canada that is the equivalent of a Certified Professional Accountant in the US) at one of the top four accounting firms in the world. It was then, in my first real place of employment, when I started to notice that things were not as equal as I had previously imagined. Although the proportions of men and women at entry- and middle-manager levels of the firm were roughly equal, most of the partners of the firm were men. I didn't look deeper into the possible imbalances, such as earning gaps or equity in the type of work men and women in similar positions were doing, but I do know now that in 1998, working women in Ontario were earning 81% of what men earned.[1]

In 1999, I relocated to London, England, and in 2003, I landed my first job in investment banking at a bank with German origins that was, at the time, the second-largest European real estate financier. It was my first foray into a male-dominated industry—real estate and investment banking. Out of eleven people, I was the only client-facing, front-office female staff member.

In my second investment banking job, in the Structured Real Estate Capital team at a Dutch bank, out of a team of about forty-five people, there were only four women, only two of whom in senior positions.

---

1   "Gender Wage Gaps and Earnings Ratios in Ontario," Pay Equity Commission, accessed April 9, 2016, http://www.payequity.gov.on.ca/en/GWG/Pages/gender_gaps_ont.aspx.

In both of these companies, women represented 9% of a client-facing workforce, even though women make up 50% of the global population.

In 2011, I relocated to Vancouver to join the impact investing team of a major credit union in Canada. With its female CEO and a board of directors that was more than 50% women, the credit union was often cited as a leader in gender equity at the leadership level. The team I joined had three women (out of eight staff) who were client-facing and made deals. This 37.5% representation by women was a remarkable improvement over the 9% I had experienced in London, but over time, I noticed that in other departments of the credit union and at the senior management level, the majority of the decision-making or client-facing staff were men.

One of the most striking things I noticed in Vancouver was how many supportive communities were focused on women. Never had I been invited to so many women-focused events and asked to join women-specific associations and networks.

I was at a point in my career where I was no longer oblivious to gender inequity. I paid more attention to articles in the media and commentary from friends and colleagues about gender inequity, particularly in the technology sector, on boards of directors of companies, and in venture capital and the investment industry. I also started to make it a practice to look for the people, the leaders, and the organizations that were doing something to create and enable more gender diversity and equity. I reached a tipping point when I met people from Criterion Institute and learned about their Women Effect Investments initiative. From Joy Anderson, the president and founder of Criterion Institute, I learned a phrase that put words to the work I was about to embark upon: "gender lens investing."

What Is Gender Lens Investing?

Gender lens investing means taking into consideration the participation, needs, realities, and leadership of both women and men when investing in businesses.

It is more than just investing in women-led businesses and women entrepreneurs. Jackie VanderBrug, Senior Vice President at US Trust, a former managing director of Criterion Ventures, and a leading voice in gender lens investing, notes that a lens means the point(s) of view by which we can analyze investments.[1] In their article in the *Stanford Social Innovation Review*, "The Rise of Gender Capitalism," VanderBrug and her coauthor Sarah Kaplan, an associate professor of strategic management at the Rotman School of Management, University of Toronto, reference Criterion Institute's Gender Handbooks for Investors.[2] VanderBrug and Kaplan note that although gender lens investing is focused on the impact on women and girls, the movement uses the term "gender" to include both men and women in the discussion and solutions. The use of the term "gender" encourages participants in the movement to look at the roles, relationships, and expectations of men and women that have been defined and shaped by social constructs. We have to look more closely at how social, cultural, political, economic, and education systems have been designed and have evolved to reinforce such social constructs. Gender lens investing goes beyond just focusing on women and challenges these deeply embedded constructs and systems.[3]

Criterion Institute, a not-for-profit research and advocacy organization based in Connecticut, is a leader in this field. It focuses on three main areas in the investment spectrum:

- **Access to capital for women:** How investment decisions, systems, and activities can direct capital toward women entrepreneurs and women-led businesses

---

1 Jackie VanderBrug, "Mainstreaming Gender Lens Investing," *Stanford Social Innovation Review*, June 12, 2012, accessed April 9, 2016, http://www.ssireview.org/articles/entry/mainstreaming_gender_lens_investing.

2 "Gender Handbook: A Guide to Understanding Gender Terms, Analysis, and Applications to Social Investing," Criterion Institute, accessed April 9, 2016, http://criterioninstitute.org/resources/files/2012/08/The-Gender-Handbook-for-Investors.pdf.

3 Sarah Kaplan and Jackie VanderBrug, "The Rise of Gender Capitalism," *Stanford Social Innovation Review*, Fall 2014, accessed April 9, 2016, http://www.ssireview.org/articles/entry/the_rise_of_gender_capitalism.

- **Gender equity in the workplace:** Looking at how investment in companies with proactive and progressive policies promoting gender equity within the company as well as in their supply chains

- **Products and services that benefit women and girls:** Focusing on investment in businesses that develop and offer products and services to a primarily female customer segment and that conduct their business in a socially responsible way that also reflects gender equity principles and values[1]

A gender lens in investing influences what kind of businesses and entrepreneurs you look for and how you evaluate them.

With a gender lens, specifically when looking at gender equity in the workplace, you may be concerned about the underrepresentation of women in certain types of businesses and industries. For example, I've read pieces in *Fast Company*, *Forbes*, and the *Washington Post* about how few computer programmers and engineers in the workforce are women, and about girls-only computer code camps. Investors and potential investors interested in investing in the technology sector with a gender lens may want to look at businesses that approach the hiring and training of women engineers in a way that encourages their development and values their perspective and contribution.

Increasing women's access to capital means investing in women-led and co-led businesses. More women investors are investing alongside groups such as Golden Seeds, which encourages greater participation by women investors. Pique Fund models itself around gender lens investing and focuses on leadership diversity. In 2016, 80% of the capital in Pique Fund was from women, the investment committee and Board are women-led, and 100% of the portfolio companies are led by CEOs who are women.The evaluation methodology used by Pique Fund has a gender lens designed into it as well.

Criterion Institute asks a number of good questions:

- **Transportation:** If we looked at transportation systems and businesses that provide transportation services (airlines, airports, car

---

1   "Gender Lens Investing," Criterion Institute, accessed April 9, 2016, http://criterioninstitute. org/revaluegender/gender-lens-investing.

sharing) with a gender lens, would we have a different view on how those services are provided (focusing more on safety, for example)?

- **Women's films and royalty structures:** How do you value slower-growth films appropriately and capture the benefits of lower risk?

- **Reproductive health, women's medical devices and services, pharmaceuticals, health care delivery:** What services are available to women? Do products and services tend to be generic rather than women-specific?

- **Big data:** How do we value the risk of less than 1% of staff in big data being women?

- **Consumer finance:** How might consumer finance be different if we invested in businesses with a gender lens?

In addition to the three primary investment objectives that Criterion Institute identifies, my gender lens is based on a hypothesis that more women providing capital positively impacts more women accessing capital. To me, gender lens investing also means improving the number of women who are investors or who make decisions about investing.

In summary, my gender lens in investing is how I evaluate investments with respect to issues of access to resources, decision-making power, and equality from my perspective as a woman.

Why Is Gender Lens Investing Important?

Nearly one hundred years after women gained their right to vote and run for political office in the US,[1] we are still talking about and dealing with issues of gender inequity, sexism, and women's rights. Conversations about women and equality range from the underrepresentation of

---

1 In the US, women gained the right to vote in 1920 with the passage of the Nineteenth Amendment to the United States Constitution, which stated, "The right of citizens of the United States to vote shall not be denied or abridged by the United States or by any State on account of sex." In Canada, women gained the right to vote in 1917, "Women's Right to Vote in Canada," Parliament of Canada, accessed April 9, 2106, http://www.parl.gc.ca/parlinfo/compilations/provinceterritory/ProvincialWomenRightToVote.aspx.

women in certain industries, on boards, and in the C-Suite to the (mis) representation of women in the media to the lack of basic human rights for women in various countries across the globe.

In 2006, Equality Now, a non-governmental organization founded in 1992 whose purpose is to work for the protection and promotion of the human rights of women and girls around the world, honored Joss Whedon for his work. In his thank-you speech he said that equality is not a concept or goal that we strive for, but rather that it is a necessity. He even compared equality to gravity—something fundamental to the existence of people on this planet. Whedon highlighted that the misogyny in almost every culture is not something that exists naturally in humankind. He made the clear statement that we all need equality. I couldn't agree more with Whedon: gender equality is a necessity, essential to the existence, survival, and happiness of people and society.

Gender lens investing is important because it is one of the ways we can effect change, level the playing field between men and women, and restore the balance in life.

In 2012, I attended an intimate conference on gender lens investing hosted by Criterion Institute. At that conference, the founder and president Joy Anderson posed the questions, "Why does gender lens investing matter?" and "What is at stake?" My answer is that diversity is at stake. Our world's survival and ability to thrive is at stake. We only have to turn to natural ecosystems to see evidence that diversity is important; without it, they cannot survive and thrive. Gender lens investing matters because it is one of the actions we can take to reverse the lack of gender equality and equity and restore diversity in our society and economy.

Examples of Diversity in Nature and How Nature Thrives

Diversity in the Temperate Rainforest:[1] Living in Vancouver places me close to the largest temperate rainforest on the planet. Observing just the plant life of the forest reveals a diverse ecosystem of living and dying flora,

---

1 "Temperate Rain Forests," World Builders, accessed April 9, 2016, http://www.world-builders. org/lessons/less/biomes/rainforest/temp_rain/temprain.html.

growing in layers of tall, medium, and low-growing and ground-loving vegetation. The tallest are the coniferous trees—most commonly, the Douglas
fir, Sitka spruce, western red cedar, and western hemlock—which reach up
to the sunlight at 130 to 280 feet. The next layer is made up of shrubs, such
as wild currants, thimbleberries, and huckleberries, that enjoy sunlight fil-
tered through the coniferous canopy. Below them grow shade-loving trees,
such as dogwoods and vine maples. On the forest floor lie dead fir needles,
twigs, leaves, and fallen trees covered by a bed of lichen, moss, grass, and
smaller plants. Mushrooms and other fungi digest, process, and recycle
the dying plant material, creating nutrient-rich soil that in turn feeds the
layers of plant life looming above. It is a beautiful cycle, made possible by
the diversity of vegetation in the forest's ecosystem.

Diversity in Animal Habitats:[1] Western parts of the us were once the
natural habitat for wolves; in the 1800s, however, settlers expanded into
these parts, tilling the land for agriculture and destroying the habitat the
wolves' natural prey needed to survive. When wolves began to prey on
domestic livestock, humans began to poison, control, and eliminate them.
Predator control was rampant. Wolves were locally extinct in Yellowstone
Park for seventy years, up until the grey wolf was reintroduced to the park
between 1994 and 1996. During the time they were absent from the park,
the population of one of their prey, the elk, grew significantly because it had
no natural predator. Despite human attempts to manage the elk population,
they increased in number and destroyed much of the park's vegetation
through their unencumbered grazing.

The reintroduction of the grey wolf not only affected the elk population
directly through kills; it also changed the elk's behavior and, in turn, changed
the landscape of Yellowstone Park. The elk began avoiding areas where they
would be at greater risk of becoming the wolves' prey, such as the valleys,
and those valleys began to regenerate with plant life and trees. With that
came the return of birds and beavers. The beavers' dam-building began to
change the infrastructure of the park's river systems, creating habitats for
other animals, and the physical geography also changed as increased vegetation prevented soil erosion and stabilized the riverbanks.

---

1 "Wolf Restoration," National Park Service, accessed April 9, 2016, https://www.nps.gov/
   yell/learn/nature/wolf-restoration.htm and *How Wolves Change Rivers*, Sustainable Human,
   accessed April 9, 2016, https://www.youtube.com/watch?v=ysa5OBhXz-Q.

The wolves killed other predators in the park such as coyotes, the carcasses of which provided food to other animals, especially those that scavenged. The changes in numbers of other predators increased the population of smaller animals like rabbits and mice, which in turn attracted hawks, weasels, and foxes. Bears thrived on scavenged food, feeding on smaller animals, wolf kills, and berries made possible by the increased plant life.

The introduction of a small number of wolves changed the ecosystem of Yellowstone Park, making room for greater diversity and the possibility of a self-managed system that required less, not more, intervention by humans.

The Connection Between Gender Lens Investing and Integrated Investing

My experience of designing and developing this new, radical, integrated investment methodology happened in parallel with my exposure to the gender lens investing community and movement. This was no coincidence, as investing with a gender lens overlaps with many of the concepts and components of integrated investing.

GENDER LENS INVESTING AND ACCESS TO ESSENTIAL RESOURCES

One of the components of integrated investing is the impact concept of access to essential resources. The question of women and their level of access to resources has come up in news articles, research papers, conference topics, and in conversation for centuries, and continues today. This includes women's right to vote and run for positions in government; the pay gap between women and men; the proportion of women in leadership positions in business and on boards; and the number of women investors as compared to men. The range of contexts include, but isn't limited to, women accessing jobs, women entrepreneurs accessing capital to start or grow their businesses, women accessing the products and services they need, and women accessing the information they need to make decisions.

By applying a gender lens, we can examine women's access to essential resources. Investing with a gender lens means that our investment choices and actions can begin to influence and address any impairment or lack of access. We can choose to invest in businesses that improve women's access to essential resources. The simple act of investing in a women-led or co-led business can in and of itself improve the women entrepreneurs' access to capital.

The presence of more women investors who speak out as influential shareholders in companies can make a difference in how products and services catering to women are made and delivered. I believe that if women grow to represent a larger proportion of the investor community and are more vocal in their investments in companies, it will make the difference between women getting what they want in products and services—being empowered and supported as customers—and being told what they should want and risking being exploited.

GENDER LENS INVESTING AND WHY WE INVEST

What motivates men and women to invest is different, and I believe investment advisors and businesses offering investment opportunities must acknowledge this.

Nelli Oster, PhD, a director and investment strategist at Black-Rock's Multi-Asset Strategies group, pointed out that women tend to focus more on longer-term goals and not all of their goals are monetary ones. As a Fidelity Investments guide[1] lays out, women generally associate money with security, independence, and the quality of their and their families' lives. According to a 2010 Boston Consulting Group study[2] examining women's experiences with wealth management providers, women tend to focus on longer-horizon planning, like college savings. Men, on the other hand, who tend to be more competitive and thrill-seeking by nature, often focus on the short-term track records of their portfolios.[3]

---

1   "Maximizing a Major Opportunity: Engaging Female Clients," Fidelity Investments, accessed April 9, 2016, https://fiiscontent.fidelity.com/954113.pdf.

2   Peter Damisch et al, "Leveling the Playing Field: Upgrading the Wealth Management Experience for Women," The Boston Consulting Group, July 2010, accessed April 9, 2016, http://www.bcg.com/documents/file56704.pdf.

3   Nelli Oster, PhD, "Men vs. Women: Investment Decisions," BlackRock Blog, February 26, 2014, accessed April 9, 2016, http://www.blackrockblog.com/2014/02/26/men-women-investment-decisions.

GENDER LENS AND IMPACT INVESTING

In Chapter 3 I introduced the idea of impact investing as taking care of the village. Observations I've made in the field of investing, as well as anecdotal evidence I have gathered, indicates that women take a more holistic view of investing than men do. They take into consideration how their decisions affect how they take care of themselves, their families, their neighbors, their communities, and the planet.

There is little hard data on gender and impact investing, but some is available through the ImpactAssets 50 database, the first publicly available database of experienced private debt and equity impact investment fund managers. This annually updated list is made up of a mix of impact venture firms, microfinance institutions, community development finance institutions, investment banks, not-for-profits, and includes organizations from around the world. The analysis provides a broad and illustrative overview of the intersection of gender and investing.

A review of the ImpactAssets 50 list in early 2016 revealed that the proportion of women in leadership teams of impact investing organizations was 35%, on a weighted average basis. (If a team of ten had three women on it, a team of five had two women, and a team of eight had three women, the weighted average would be eight out of twenty-three, or 34.8%). The weighted average proportion of women on leadership teams appears to be higher than in conventional venture firms, as noted below, and the representation of women on leadership and senior executive teams is diverse, ranging from 0% to 100%. Though the ImpactAssets 50 list is not a comprehensive list of all debt and equity impact investment organizations, it hints at the low representation of women in impact investment leadership teams (compared to the proportion that women make up of the global population).

Some impact investing teams, however, are made up of 100% women, a statistic that is rare in the conventional and traditional investment industry. This may indicate that there are opportunities for women in the impact space, or that impact investing and its variations are more welcoming or attractive to women compared to more traditional firms.

Barbara Stewart, a portfolio manager in Toronto who advises high-net-worth individuals and families, conducted research focusing on women and finance by asking a hundred women how they spend their personal time, energy, and money, and published her findings in her "Rich Thinking" white paper series.[1] She found that the traditional investment model, based on asset classes (that is, equities, bonds, real estate, and cash), did not tell the whole story. Barbara remarked that some women invested in houses, not necessarily focusing on a potential investment return, but rather because houses gave the women a sense of security and feeling of warmth. She also noted that women also invested in their personal causes that gave them a deeper sense of meaning and feeling of doing what is important to them.

Barbara found that women are investing in their families and spending time and energy on them. I was particularly intrigued by her findings that women seek to make a difference in parallel with their daily activities and livelihoods. She also noted that women are investing in themselves by spending time, energy, and money on things that matter to them and enable them to thrive—be it intellectual stimulation, physical challenge, or a way of expressing themselves. Because of this, the traditional model of making a lot of money and then doing something good—philanthropy or angel and venture investing, for example—doesn't necessarily work for women.

By and large, **women are integrating their activities of investing in their families, personal causes, and their selves into their lives and activities as they go along.** Barbara's findings align with the concept of taking care of the village. I am inclined to believe that an integrated approach to investing resonates with *women and that they could very well be naturals at impact investing.*

GENDER LENS AND VALUES

I struggled to write this section because I wondered if there was a gender lens to our values. I'd like to think we have values in common, irrespective of our gender—values such as freedom, justice, equality, and harmony, to name just a few. However, thinking about it further, I realized that even these values highlight how we are all informed by our gender lens and perspective.

1   Barbara Stewart, "Rich Thinking," accessed June 11, 2016, http://barbarastewart.ca/richthinking.html.

Women have had to fight for the freedoms most of their male coun-terparts have always had. From women's suffrage to fighting for the right to own property, have a bank account, or borrow money, there are many examples of women not being treated equally or equitably with men over the course of history. As such, there are things that I value because I am a woman, and I have had certain experiences men have not had as a result of being a woman.

For example, consider women in technology, one of the industries in which I work and look for potential investment opportunities. Many women I know who are entrepreneurs working and operating in the technology sector value gender diversity and equity in their sector because it affects how they and their colleagues are treated, it affects what kind of access to opportunities and investment capital they have, and it can affect the progress and success of their ventures. I have heard a real-life story of a male investor who turned away a female CEO because he did not invest in women with young children.

Gender Diversity in Technology Companies

Does having a female CEO make a difference? At Yahoo, 37% of global employees are women, but women fill only 16% of tech roles and 25% of leadership positions.

	Global	Tech	Non-tech	Leadership	Source
Google	30%	18%	47%	22%	1
Facebook	32%	16%	52%	23%	2
Twitter	34%	13%	50%	22%	3
Yahoo	37%	16%	54%	24%	4
Salesforce	30%	23%	32%	19%	5
LinkedIn	42%	18%	50%	30%	6
Pinterest	42%	21%	66%	16%	7

1 https://www.google.com/diversity/
2 http://newsroom.fb.com/news/2015/06/driving-diversity-at-facebook/
3 https://blog.twitter.com/2015/we-re-committing-to-a-more-diverse-twitter
4 https://yahoo.tumblr.com/post/123472998984/please-see-here-for-our-eeo-1-report
5 http://www.salesforce.com/company/careers/diversity-numbers.jsp
6 https://blog.linkedin.com/2015/06/08/linkedins-2015-workforce-diversity
7 https://blog.pinterest.com/en/our-plan-more-diverse-pinterest

This table shows diversity data reported in 2015. URLs accessed on April 11, 2016.

But it is not just the technology sector where this is true. Gender diversity and equity is an issue in various industries—media and entertainment, financial services, sports, the medical professions, and politics, among others. The issues that matter to you shape your values. If the gender-based issues experienced in these industries and areas are important to you, then these issues will influence your decisions and actions.

Equal pay and opportunities for women in industry may be one of your values. Maternal health and women's rights with respect to their bodies may be another. Women's right to vote and hold office may be one as well. A gender lens can be applied to all of these issues and more because women and men have historically been treated differently in these areas, and this different treatment continues today.

In 1995, Ann M. Beutel and Margaret Mooney Marini, both professors at the University of Minnesota at that time, conducted research on gender and values. They examined three measures of values: 1) compassion, which reflects concern and responsibility for the well-being of others; 2) materialism, which reflects emphasis on material benefit and competition; and 3) meaning, which reflects philosophical concern with finding purpose and meaning in life.

They found that men and women differed on all three measures. Amongst the people involved in the study, women were more likely than men to express concern and responsibility for the well-being of others; less likely to accept materialism and competition; and more likely to indicate that finding purpose and meaning in life is extremely important. Beutel and Marini observed these gender differences over a period from the mid-1970s to the early 1990s. They found these trends were evident irrespective of social class, religion, or the perceived avail-ability of social support.[1]

This is research from just one study, and an old study at that, but its findings continue to hold true today: what is important to women is often different from what is important to men, and that shapes their values, which in turn affects their decision making.

Making the Case for Gender Lens Investing

We often hear women being spoken about as an untapped market or underutilized resource. We hear that women control a significant amount of wealth in the world, and that this share is ever-growing. This kind of language appears in the finance industry all the time. From a business perspective, herein lies the case for gender lens investing.

Businesses are increasingly being encouraged to hire more women for roles where they are underrepresented, and their boards of direc-tors are being encouraged to include more women. This is because the business world is finally realizing the importance of understanding how women make economic decisions as business and community leaders and the value that women contribute to the process of making critical business decisions.

We hear about initiatives that engage more women, but what does this actually mean to you as an investor? Simple: it can mean better returns and outcomes.

BETTER RETURNS

Illuminate Ventures, a high-tech venture capital firm based in the San Francisco area managed by Cindy Padnos, published a white paper in 2010 that stated the following:

- Women build more capital-efficient businesses, using less capital to achieve the same or higher levels of success as their male counterparts.

- Women-led ventures experienced lower failure rates.

- Women-led ventures are able to achieve venture-level returns.

---

1   Ann M. Beutel and Margaret Mooney Marini, "Gender and Values," *American Sociological Review*, Vol. 60 (June 1995): 436-448.

- Gender diversity improves performance.

- If female-led ventures perform just as well as (or better than) their male-led counterparts, why is it that less than 10% of venture capital investment goes to female-led ventures? Illuminate Ventures makes the case that it is time to invest in women-led businesses.

Meredith Jones is an alternative investment consultant and the author of *Women of the Street: Why Female Money Managers Generate Higher Returns (and How You Can Too)*. She has been researching and writing about women investors since 2012, focusing on managers of alternative investment funds. She developed the Kass Women in Alternative Investments (WAI) Hedge Fund Index, a metric used to track the performance of a group of women-run hedge funds and measure how well the funds are doing year after year. In her 2013 white paper, "Women in Alternative Investments: A Marathon, Not a Sprint," she found that for the six and a half years ending in June 2013, the WAI Hedge Fund Index performed better than the S&P 500, a US stock market index based on the 500 largest companies listed on the New York Stock Exchange or on NASDAQ and the HFRX Global Hedge Fund Index, an index of over forty hedge funds, created by Hedge Fund Research Inc.[1]

GREATER IMPACT

The benefits of investing with a gender lens go beyond financial returns. It helps elevate women as leaders and creates new role models, shapes what products and services are created, helps businesses determine how to serve people better, and paves a path toward diversity.

Deloitte, an international advisory and services firm, published "The Gender Dividend: Making the Business Case for Investing in Women" in 2011. In its paper, Deloitte quotes Scott Page, professor of complex systems theory at the University of Michigan, who says that when it comes to solving complex problems or innovating, a diverse group of competent performers almost always outperforms a homogenous

---

1   The Kass Women in Alternative Investments Hedge Fund Index returned 6%, while the S&P 500 gained 4.2% and the HFRX Global Hedge Fund Index dropped 1.1% during the same period.

group of star performers by a substantial margin.[1] The authors of "The Gender Dividend" encourage collaboration amongst men and women, citing that the real power is in collaboratively using their respective strengths and experience to solve complex problems and innovate.[2]

The Rise of Women Investors

Women as investors are an important aspect of a gender lens. We haven't heard a lot about women's successes and experiences as investors in the media in the past, but that is changing now.

Women and Wealth

Global business consulting firm Boston Consulting Group published their findings from a 2010 study they conducted.[3] In it, they discuss how women controlled an estimated 27% (or $20 trillion) of the world's wealth in 2009, and North America and Western Europe accounted for more than two-thirds (or $14.3 trillion). This amount was expected to grow at an average annual rate of 8% from 2009 to 2014.

This has resulted from a number of factors, including greater activity by women in the workforce, increased involvement of women in managing household finances, women's longer life expectancy, and the increasing amount of wealth women are inheriting.

From 1980 to 2008, the number of women in the global workforce doubled to 1.2 billion. Although an income gap between men and women still exists (a woman earns, on average, $0.77 for every dollar a man earns), the gap has declined over time. As it has, the proportion of women whose wealth is entirely self-earned has increased.

Meanwhile, more women are also inheriting wealth today. According to Boston College's Center on Wealth and Philanthropy, women will inherit 70% of the $41 trillion in intergenerational wealth transfer expected by 2050.

---

1   Scott Page, *The Difference: How the Power of Diversity Creates Better Groups, Firms, Schools and Societies* (Princeton University Press, 2007).

2   Greg Pellegrino et al, "The Gender Dividend: Making the Business Case for Investing in Women," Deloitte, 2011.

3   Damisch et al, "Levelling the Playing Field."

Women and Angel Investing

In their annual study of angel investors in the US, the Center for Venture Research at the University of New Hampshire found that, in 2015, 25.3% of angel investors in the US were women. Five years earlier, it was estimated that less than 5% of angel investors in Europe were women.

EBAN, the European Trade Association for Business Angels, Seed Funds and Early Stage Market Players, has hypothesized about how the angel investment sector would benefit if 20% of angel investors were women. EBAN believes that the total number of angel investors would increase, leading to an increase in the amount of investment and number of deals being funded. They also believe that a more diverse investor base would attract a wider array of underrepresented business propositions in the areas of services, consumer goods, and social and sustainable entrepreneurship, diversifying beyond just high-technology businesses. It could also lead to diversified expertise for funded businesses. Angel investors provide more than just money to the businesses they invest in—they bring expertise, experience, and a network of contacts to support their investment—and more women investors could mean the possibility of tapping into a more diverse base of knowledge and expertise. All of this could lead to societies and economies that grow and thrive better, more sustainably and with greater diversity.

In 2010, EBAN researched why there are so few women investors in Europe. These are their findings:

- Women tend to underestimate their financial capacity for risky investments.

- Women perceive angel investing as requiring a large capital outlay.

- Women's myriad of duties with family and community impact their schedules differently than those of men, and they may rely on professional advisors or investment funds when it comes to wealth management in an effort to save time and energy.

- Because of their different backgrounds and skill sets, women come to angel investing differently than men.

- Women lack exposure to the asset class of venture.

- There is a lack of established cohorts of women business angels.

- Current services in the angel network industry are marketed by men, for men, to men.

- Women are less likely to be networked to other investors.

While there is not a lot of research into why there are disproportionately fewer women investors compared to men in the US, possible reasons are likely similar to those uncovered in the European research. Many people like to hypothesize that women lack the risk appetite or the financial capacity to become angel investors. Women are risk aware; however, there may be some truth to the disadvantage in lack of financial capacity. Typically, angel investors have come into their money as successful entrepreneurs who sold their stake in their businesses, or as well-paid executives of successful companies. But if women are not able to access the same financial and business opportunities as men as a result of systemic gender inequity, then it makes sense that there would be a domino effect, resulting in fewer women investing or fewer investment dollars controlled by women.

Here are some of the reasons I believe there are few well-known women investors:

- Women are more private about their investing activity.

- Women are clubbing together to invest, resulting in fewer single investors that stand out.

- Many women, even those with considerable wealth and expertise do not meet accredited investor definitions and are therefore structurally excluded from angel investing.

- Women are seeking investment opportunities that provide multiple outcomes (economic, social, environmental), and the investments they do make are not regularly reported in the media at the moment.

- Women are making small investments in others and in their communities, and these types of single investments do not capture the attention of the general venture community.

I don't believe there are fewer well-known female angel investors because they are risk adverse and poorer in technology and business skills. I believe women investors simply make decisions differently than men do, and they are showing up in the investment sector differently. I do believe we could benefit from more women actively and visibly participating as investors in a way that plays to women's strengths, is appealing and attractive to women, and makes room for different definitions of value and success. If we could achieve this, we'd have more diverse investment decisions and a more diverse economic environment—and diversity of perspectives is critical to a healthy, thriving economy.

If we look at how venture investment opportunities are brought to investors, we observe that the current offerings tend to meet the preferences of the predominantly male audience. Where and when angel investors meet may not suit women's needs and time preferences. The current angel investment community does not support an investment scale that fits women's spectrum of financial capacity. The community is also lacking in a support structure that would help women to understand best practices as they invest.

We can enable more women to participate in society and the economic system as investors by enabling an investment culture and investment structures that serve women. We should be paying attention to and valuing how women make decisions about their time, energy, and money. The investment industry needs to consider investment structures that work for people with the financial capacity, risk appetite, and acumen to invest, but who do not meet accredited investor definitions. Most of the women I have spoken with who are interested in investing are busy working, teaching, supporting their causes, and spending time with their friends and families. Time is precious, and they want to spend it wisely. If they are going to spend time on investing activities, they want to do so while having fun and meeting interesting people in a dynamic, social environment. If the investment industry is going to attract more women, it needs to create investing experiences that have these qualities.

The more women who are exposed to investing mentors and role models, the more believe that investing is for them. Immersion in an investment community is another way to learn the ropes of investing and join in. Some investors are more private about their investments and don't want their investing activities to be visible. We need to think about creating a safe environment and investing experience that respects this privacy, yet enables newer investors to connect with others who are actively investing so they can learn from them and be mentored.

Giving people access to the right information, tools, and resources can help them become more active as investors. Whether it is understanding how the investment process works or finding opportunities that feel meaningful and purposeful, having access to information, tools, and resources that are delivered in a values-aligned way is critical for helping investors develop and grow. We need to do more to make investor education and training resources more accessible to women.

Women, Gender Lens Investing, and Integrated Decision Making

The integrated decision making approach I described in Chapter 5 asserts that optimal investment decisions result when people integrate analysis, emotion, body, and intuition into their decision-making process. When I've shared my approach with men, many have said they are curious about it or find it interesting; when I've shared it with women, I've received knowing nods. It is resoundingly women who empathize with integrated decision making, some even describing it as a feminine approach.

While I believe everyone benefits from integrated investing, perhaps it will be women who lead the way. In my opinion, women are naturals at integrated decision making and integrated investing. Just as we are seeing changes in business and society, with more and more women starting and growing businesses and in senior management and leadership positions, we may start to see more and more women investors in the years to come.

Summary

I believe diversity benefits our economy and society, but the investment industry has a bad track record for gender diversity. It's time for change, and that takes time. If we recognize and celebrate women who are already leading the way as investors, however, and continue to create communities and environments that support how women invest and what they want to invest in, I believe a better gender balance—and perhaps even gender equity—is possible.

IN CLOSING

NOW THAT YOU have read about the foundational pieces of access to essential resources, why we invest, impact investing, values, integrated decision making, and mindsets, and about the practical tools in the integrated investing toolkit, investment relationships, and gender lens investing, it is time to put integrated investing into practice.

Here are some final thoughts and guidance on how to put each of the parts of this book to use in your own investing activities.

1. Start Looking at Investing Through the Lens of Access to Essential Resources

To survive, thrive, and be happy, there are certain things in life we all want and need. These can be placed into six categories of essential resources:

1. Sustenance
2. Expression
3. Connection
4. Managing change
5. Making decisions
6. Exchange

Purposeful businesses give us six different types of access to essential resources:

1. Basic access
2. More efficient access
3. Access to more or better choices of resources
4. More convenient access
5. Access through the supply chain
6. Access through employment

Looking at businesses and investing through the lens of access to essential resources enables you to see the potential impact in investment opportunities you may not have seen before. You may also start to realize the value of certain businesses that you may have previously overlooked as investment opportunities.

With this focus, you move beyond just looking at specific impact segments or sectors such as food, energy, and microfinance, and you begin to take a more holistic approach. You will consider whether a business provides access to one or more essential resources that people need to survive, thrive, and be happy before investing in it.

A business may provide multiple types of resources through different types of access. Practice looking at businesses from different angles, and some resources that are not as obvious as others might start to reveal themselves.

Impact is the improvement in access to essential resources. This change in perspective provides the starting point for evaluating impact investment opportunities. By thinking about access, you can begin to develop an understanding of how the businesses in which you could invest are connected with the things in life that people need to survive, thrive, and be happy.

2. Reflect on Why You Invest

Reflecting upon why you invest involves asking about the context of your investments: "Why do I do what I do?" What is it that motivates you to invest? What is your desired outcome?

Investing can provide you with access to these essential resources:

• Sustenance by providing you with an income stream or financial returns

- Expression, such as power, status, or leadership
- Connection, such as connecting with other investors and with the entrepreneurs in which you could invest
- Managing change by providing security, an opportunity for future consumption, preparation for obsolescence, innovation, or legacy
- Making decisions
- Exchange

Reflect on the times you have invested in impact ventures in the past—or, if you are new to impact investing, think about your journey up to this point. Then practice telling the story of your experience of investing, or the path you've traveled to get here, to other people. This will help you articulate why you invest. Being clear on this question of why helps you clarify for yourself what outcomes you expect from your investing activities.

3. Get More Resources on Impact Investing

The phrase "impact investing" was coined in 2007, but as a field it continues to grow and evolve. Impact is described by some people in the impact investing industry as solving social or environmental problems or challenges or generating measurable social and environmental impact, but I think of impact as an improvement in access to essential resources. When we improve access to essential resources, we achieve the following effects:

- Empowering people and the planet (rather than exploiting them)
- Creating more equal societies
- Taking care of the village

We are all better off when we treat investing as a way to take care of the village. To deepen your knowledge about impact investing, I highly recommend continuing to read about impact investing and related subjects; I guarantee doing so will change the way you think about investing. You can start with these three resources:

- Stanford Social Innovation Review: www.ssireview.org/topics/category/impact_investing

- Global Impact Investing Network: www.thegiin.org
- Impact Alpha: www.impactalpha.com

Additional resources are included in the Further Reading section of this book.

4. Put Your Investments to the Values Test

If you are clear on what your values are and what is important to you, put your investments to the values test. If you're unsure of what values are most important to you, go back to Chapter 4 and do the exercise included there; it should help you articulate your values.

It's crucial to understand how your values align with access to essential resources, because your values influence which types of access and which types of resources are most important to you. It's also important to think about how your values align with and influence your motivations for investing.

Ask yourself whether the companies and products in which you are investing reflect your values or if they are in conflict with them. If they are in conflict, start to think about what types of companies and investments would better suit your interests and align with your beliefs. This will help you shape your investment strategy and criteria so they're more aligned with your values.

5. Practice Integrated Decision Making

Analysis helps us make decisions; however, emotion inevitably affects our investment decisions, and greater emotional awareness can actually help us make better decisions. Our bodies can also affect how we approach risk or stress, and therefore play a part in our investment decisions. Intuition is necessary for making decisions in the face of uncertainty, which is particularly important in investing.

Integrating information from analysis, emotion, body, and intuition will help you more quickly and confidently make decisions about how you want to move forward with an investment opportunity.

Integrated decision making is something you can practice every day, and not only regarding investing. Start by practicing with simpler decisions; check in on your analysis, your emotions, your body, and your intuition before reaching a conclusion. Then progress to more complicated and complex decisions. Your decisions are optimized if your head, heart, body, and soul are in sync. If they are not, your decision will reflect the path you chose, whether it was led by analysis, emotion, body, or intuition. Being aware of what leads your decision helps you be prepared for the outcome.

Once you've become comfortable with the process, practice applying integrated decision making to your investment decisions. Rather than excluding emotions, body, and intuition from your investment decisions, be aware of inputs from these areas, and incorporate them into your decision alongside analysis; this will help you make more integrated decisions.

Before making an investment decision, ask yourself the following questions:

1. What do I think I should do?
2. What do I want to do?
3. What signals is my body giving me?
4. What would I intuitively do?

6. Practice the New Mindsets

To prepare and be ready for integrated investing, put yourself in the right mindset for it.

In Chapter 6, I discussed six groups of mindsets, divided into three categories:

- Mindsets that affect your perception about resources and risk:
  - Abundance and scarcity
  - Curiosity and fear

- Mindsets that influence your outlook on how to relate to and interact with others:

- · Exchange, self-interest, and serving others
- · Relationship and transaction

- Mindsets that affect your frame of mind about results:
  - · Future potential and past performance
  - · Resources and money

Rather than focusing on scarcity, risk, self-interest, transaction, past performance, and money, integrated investing focuses on abundance, curiosity, exchange, relationship, future potential, and resources. By focusing on these more open, positive, and inviting mindsets, you will be more receptive to the possibilities available to you, which will allow you to achieve more positive impact in your investing activities.

Before making any impact investing decisions, pause and reflect upon what mindset you're in. If you realize you're experiencing some of the more closed-off mindsets of scarcity, risk, self-interest, transaction, past performance, and money, think about the complementary mindset in those mindsets' pairings or groups. For instance, if you're feeling a scarcity mindset, take a breath and imagine an abundance mindset. Say out loud what is abundant to help you get yourself into that mindset; then, once you've achieved a change in perspective, revisit the decision and observe whether a different approach or decision can be taken. Make your decisions and act with mindsets of abundance, curiosity, exchange, relationship, future potential, and resources.

7. Apply the Integrated Investing Toolkit

In Chapter 7 I shared the practical tips and tools you can apply to your investment activities in order to identify and evaluate impactful investment opportunities. By combining traditional investment evaluation tools, venture development and evaluation tools, and impact identification and evaluation tools, you give yourself a complete set of processes and methods for evaluating impact investment opportunities.

The integrated investing toolkit helps you gather the information needed for integrated decision making when you are presented with an investment opportunity. Bear in mind that access to essential resources, your motivations for investing, your values, and your mindsets all affect your decision making. Keep these foundational pieces and techniques in mind as you gather the information you need through application of the integrated investing toolkit.

The knowledge you have, your awareness of risk and impact, and the information you collect through your application of the integrated investing toolkit will lead you to the exciting point of making an investment decision.

8. Join Other People Who Are Investing

Integrated investing requires practice. When you're new to impact investing, joining a community, network, or group of like-minded people that can support you and collaborate with you is a great place to start.

Impact investing is not just a transaction; it is an investment relationship (recall the relationship mindset from Chapter 6). Remember that building relationships with entrepreneurs takes time. Look for someone you feel a desire to work with—and who wants to work with you as well—and don't be afraid to ask tough questions. You want to be able to make it through good times and bad with the entrepreneur you're investing in. Be clear about what you're looking for in the investment relationship. As in any relationship, there should be both give and take, and you want the relationship to feel fair and balanced.

Impact investing can be an exciting opportunity to meet other investors and entrepreneurs involved in impact ventures, and to invest in and build meaningful, purposeful businesses of the future together.

9. Consider Investing with a Gender Lens

Gender lens investing means taking into consideration the participation, needs, realities, and leadership of both women and men when evaluating businesses for the purposes of investing.

Gender equality in investing is important because it is one of the ways we can effect change, level the playing field amongst men and women, and restore the balance in life. Diversity is natural in living systems like the rainforest and animal habitats; it should be just as natural in human systems, business and investing included.

This book opened with a discussion of the things in life we all want and need to survive, thrive, and be happy. Gender lens investing matters because it is one of the actions we can take to reverse the lack of gender equality and equity, and to restore diversity, which enables thriving and happier societies and economies.

The next time you evaluate an investment opportunity, do so with a gender lens. Reflect on how the participation, needs, realities, and leadership of both women and men are affected by the business you're evaluating. Take gender equality and diversity into consideration before you make your next investment decision.

Final Thoughts

If we are going to really change the landscape of investing and have a positive impact on the world around us, we need to change how we think about investing and how we make investment decisions.

This change starts with looking at the products and services we buy and the activities we undertake—including investing—as more than just things we consume. These products, services, and activities are essential resources we need to survive, thrive, and be happy. For essential resources to exist, we need to invest in the businesses that give us access to them.

We need to think again about why we invest in the first place and about how our investing activities and investment choices express our values and align with them. We can be more holistic about how we make investment decisions and use all the inputs available to us. That means integrating inputs from analysis, emotion, body, and intuition into our investment decisions. We need to shift our mindsets before we invest.

These are profound changes. I hope integrated investing helps you take a step closer toward investing for positive impact with head, heart, body, and soul.

FURTHER READING

COMPILED HERE IS a list of books and resources that I've found helpful. Some are directly related to specific chapters of integrated investing, while others are interesting reads that could expand your worldview and be useful in your evaluation of impact and in your investment decisions.

The field of impact investing is growing and evolving. It pays to gather more information and practice continuous learning. Here are some resources to help you do that.

For further guidance on how to categorize opportunities into one or more of the six essential resources discussed in Chapter 1, refer to the Essential Resources Chart on the Integrated Investing website at integratedinvesting.ca. On the chart, I've listed areas of business and investment ranging from food to financial services to information and placed checkmarks under one or more essential resources that are applicable.

For further insights on the subject of motivations in a broader context, the RSA (Royal Society for the encouragement of Arts, Manufactures and Commerce) featured a great video[1] through their RSA Animate series called *Drive*, based on the critically acclaimed book of

---

[1] *Drive: The Surprising Truth About What Motivates Us*, The RSA, accessed April 14, 2016, https://www.youtube.com/watch?v=u6XAPnuFjJc

the same name by Daniel Pink (Riverhead Books, 2009). Pink provides useful insight on three elements of motivation—autonomy, mastery, and purpose.

On investing as taking care of the village and to deepen your knowledge on the issues of income and wealth inequality, dig deeper into Richard Wilkinson and Kate Pickett's *The Spirit Level* (Penguin, 2010). A much heavier tome on the subject of capital and inequality is *Capital in the Twenty-First Century* (Belknap, 2014), written by French economist Thomas Piketty. Some of Piketty's theories could be challenged, but the historical account of capital and income is certainly helpful for understanding some of the principles that underlie present-day issues. *Prosperity Without Growth* (Earthscan Publications, 2009) by Tim Jackson, a professor of sustainable development, is a daring book that challenges the concept of unfettered economic growth and considers how to sustain human prosperity and well-being in the future.

On the topic of integrated decision making (Chapter 5), *Eyes Wide Open* (HarperBusiness, 2013) by economist Noreena Hertz encourages us to be more discerning and empowered in our decision making. *Blink* (Back Bay Books, 2007) by popular author Malcolm Gladwell is an easy introduction to concepts of rapid cognition, intuition, and quick decision making. *The Intuitive Investor* (Select Books, 2010) is written by Jason Voss, CFA and former Wall Street investment manager, and is one of the rare sources that talks about mindfulness and spirituality in the context of money management. An interesting book that links human instincts and social behavior to economic decisions is *Basic Instincts* (Marshall Cavendish Corporation, 2010) by Pete Lunn. Lunn points out that altruism and fairness, not only profit-maximizing self-interest, have strong influences on economic decisions. Lastly, *Between the Hour of Dog and Wolf* (Random House Canada, 2012) by Wall Street trader turned neuroscientist, John Coates, provides insight on how our bodies and our physiology affects risk taking and decision making, with examples from the financial industry.

Mind Set! (HarperCollins Publishers, 2006) by John Naisbitt suggests ways to open your mind to understand today's world and reveal the opportunities of the future. It was the first book that exposed me to the idea of mindset change. It provided me with a basis for recognizing mindsets (which are discussed in Chapter 6) and how they impact our thinking and decision making.

We can thank the Lean Startup movement for all the amazing and useful resources for entrepreneurs making their venture ideas a reality. *The Lean Startup* (Crown Business, 2011) by Eric Ries is the go-to book for starting a venture. It often goes hand-in-hand with *Business Model Generation* (Wiley, 2010) by Alexander Osterwalder and Yves Pigneur, and *The Four Steps to the Epiphany* (K&S Ranch, 2005) by Steve Blank. John Mullins, a professor at the London School of Business wrote two useful books, *The New Business Road Test* (Financial Times/Prentice Hall, 2003) and *Getting to Plan B* (Harvard Business School Press, 2009), coauthored with Randy Komisar. An example due diligence checklist can be found on the Integrated Investing website at integratedinvesting.ca.

There are a number of references in Chapter 9 to Criterion Institute, a not-for-profit research and advocacy organization based in Connecticut and a leader in gender lens investing. I found my community amongst the people that Criterion Institute convened for their Convergence events over the course of 2011 to 2014, focused on gender lens investing. Joy Anderson and Criterion Institute continue to be my go-to resource for the space where finance and gender intersect. You can find a wealth of resources on gender and investing at their website at https://criterioninstitute.org/revaluegender/ (last accessed April 10, 2016). Meredith A. Jones has been researching and writing about women in alternative investments for several years and her first book, *Women of the Street* (Palgrave Macmillan, 2015), offers a rare perspective in gender lens investing by focusing on female money managers.

There are more books than I have listed above that have informed the development of integrated investing. The suggestions here offer great insights, unusual perspectives, and a good starting point for understanding the landscape that influences impact investing.

ACKNOWLEDGEMENTS

THIS BOOK HAS drawn from my experience as a financier, as an investor in startups for good, and as the founder of Pique Ventures and Pique Fund. With that in mind, I want to thank MyBestHelper, Wearable Therapeutics, Beanworks Solutions, and ePact Network and the incredible CEOs that founded and lead these companies. They are all amazing early-stage companies that make a difference in the world through their products, services, and business culture. It's an honor to have the opportunity to invest in them through Pique Fund and work with the great women who lead them. Thank you in particular to Catherine Dahl, whose story I've included in brief in this book.

We put the integrated investing tools into practice in Pique Fund's investment activities and I thank Crystal Lo for helping to put them to the test.

I gratefully acknowledge Satya Patel for granting permission to quote his blog article about emotional resonance in Chapter 5.

Thank you to participants of the integrated investing course for providing feedback on the course content that was largely drawn from this book.

I am thankfully surrounded by social innovators, entrepreneurs, change makers, and impact investors that I'm honored to call colleagues, friends, and trusted advisors, in particular Servane Mouazan, David Hodgson, and Joy Anderson. Not only did they review, advise on, or comment on parts of the book, but they also do amazing work that inspires me to continue on this often complex and challenging path.

Writing in the financial industry is often technical and full of jargon that makes it opaque to most people. Thank you to Lauren Bacon for introducing me to Brooke Warner. Many thanks to Brooke for coaching me and reviewing my writing as it unfolded. Her experience and advice helped me evolve my writing and she encouraged me to take a stand.

Thank you to Lally Rementilla, the first investor and my fellow board member in Pique Fund. Working with Lally and talking through exciting opportunities, as well as tough investment decisions, with her has helped me be a better investor. It was my hope that what I've learned over the past few years could be shared through this book.

The biggest supporter of my writing endeavors is my lovely husband, who put up with many Sundays spent apart as I wrote in our local cafés. I thank him for reading drafts of my manuscript, for engaging in countless conversations about my work, investing, and current affairs, and for distracting our young daughter from the shiny screen of my computer as I worked.

ABOUT THE AUTHOR

A N IMPACT INVESTOR and alternative investment manager, Bonnie Foley-Wong is the founder of Pique Ventures and founding investor of Pique Fund.

Foley-Wong began her career as an auditor with a Big 4 accounting firm, after receiving a Bachelor of Mathematics degree and a Master of Accounting degree from the University of Waterloo. She spent twelve years in London as a corporate finance advisor and investment banker, then as an advisor to entrepreneurs and impact investors. With over two decades' experience in finance, investment banking and venture capital, Foley-Wong has financed over $1 billion of alternative investments in Europe and North America.

Foley-Wong is a Chartered Public Accountant, Chartered Accountant, and CFA charterholder. She presently resides in Vancouver, Canada, with her husband and young daughter.